Battling the Hamster Wheel™

Battling

STRATEGIES FOR MAKING

the

HIGH SCHOOL REFORM

Hamster

WORK

Wheel™

GRACE SAMMON

CORWIN PRESS
A SAGE Publications Company
Thousand Oaks, California

For information:

Corwin Press
A Sage Publications Company
2455 Teller Road
Thousand Oaks, California 91320
www.corwinpress.com

Sage Publications Ltd.
1 Oliver's Yard
55 City Road
London EC1Y 1SP
United Kingdom

Sage Publications India Pvt. Ltd.
B-42, Panchsheel Enclave
Post Box 4109
New Delhi 110 017 India

Library of Congress Cataloging-in-Publication Data

Sammon, Grace M.
Battling the hamster wheel™: Strategies for making high school reform work / Grace Sammon.
    p. cm.
Includes bibliographical references and index.
ISBN 1-4129-1782-4 (cloth)—ISBN 1-4129-1783-2 (pbk.)
   1. Education, Secondary—Aims and objectives—United States. 2. Educational change—United States. 3. School management and organization—United States. I. Title.
LB1607.5.S26 2006
373.12′00973—dc22

                                          2005014817

This book is printed on acid-free paper.

05   06   07   08   09   10 9 8 7 6 5 4 3 2 1

Acquisitions Editor:	Elizabeth Brenkus
Editorial Assistants:	Candice L. Ling and Desirée Enayati
Production Editor:	Laureen Shea
Copy Editor:	Diana Breti
Typesetter:	C&M Digitals (P) Ltd.
Proofreader:	Sally M. Scott
Indexer:	Kay Dusheck
Cover Designer:	Rose Storey

Contents

Preface

This book was born out of the frustrations I share with educators across the country regarding the limited success of the high school improvement process. *Battling the Hamster Wheel* introduces you to scenarios typical of schools in the throes of change and to my personal dilemma as an educator and consultant: how to help push a faculty past the point where they are spinning their wheels, going nowhere. As you will see, the idea for this book came in a thunderclap moment. The image was clear! Hardworking committee members, albeit well-intentioned, were like hamsters, running hard on their wheel and making no progress. What made the moment worse for me was that I realized I had jumped up on the wheel with them! *Whirr! Whirr! Whirr!*

As an educator, school reformer, consultant, speaker, and author, I have now spent nearly 20 years working in what I consider to be one of this country's most challenging institutions, the American high school. Over time, working in 32 states, like many of you, I have seen reform initiatives come and go. I have witnessed and partnered with educators working hard and meeting with varying levels of success. I have had the great privilege of participating in the national debate focusing on the status of the American high school. It is clear that at no time in the history of education have the stakes been raised so high—to educate *all* of America's children.

Educators at the federal, state, district, school, and classroom level, as well as researchers, technical assistance providers, and community groups, are all grappling with how to make their reform initiatives work. Gates, Carnegie, Annenberg, Kellogg, and an array of other national and local funders are pumping billions of dollars into high schools. The U.S. Department of Education has already released more than $647 million specifically to address the redesign of high schools into smaller learning communities.

Educators are working as hard as they can, but too often they are engaged in a system that nurtures a carousel cycle of reforms that inhibits them from making the progress the reforms seek to attain. Teachers are deeply committed to student success. However, many are working in systems that do not provide a framework that allows them to excel at the craft of teaching *today's* students. Schools are suffering from what Arnold Fege, director of Public Engagement for the Public Education Network, calls "innovation fatigue." As schools fight for reform, they are grappling with a challenge that makes them feel that perhaps all students can't learn and maybe all schools can't succeed. They enter into a cycle that lowers their expectations for success and maintains the status quo of poor outcomes for too many of our students. The belief systems, the practices and policies, and the automatic responses that make up high school culture have not helped schools meet with success.

I have worked in urban, suburban, rural, and Indian nation schools. Regardless of the venue, the questions are the same: how do we increase achievement, increase personalization, develop professional communities, and create successful learning environments for our students? The available research, data, and documented best practices provide straightforward answers, especially for our most challenged schools. However, the culture of schools, particularly high schools, has made them increasingly resistant to change.

Half of our nation's African American student population, 40% of our Latino student population, and 11% of our white student population attend high schools where graduation is not the norm. One in 20 high school students nationally do not finish high school, and 40% of those entering college need remediation. Twenty-three of the 30 fastest growing job areas require a college degree. We can no longer, if we ever could, stand by and not wrestle with the very difficult issues of why we are not succeeding for all students.

Hamster Wheel argues that the data, the students, and our own observations tell us that we need a solid, systemic approach to effective reform. This reform begins with a commitment to continuous improvement of educational practice that will require constant change, knowing and using our data, moving us to a clear mission, and developing the capacity of the educators and community leaders to meet with success. We're all working as hard as we can. We are balancing multiple, and sometimes competing, demands and initiatives. We want our organizations to meet with success, but all too often we are working in an environment that puts us on a "hamster wheel." Like those cute little pets that spend their lives running in place and jumping on and off their wheels, we are running as fast as we can on a wheel; we are not on a road to success.

My message is a hard one to hear and acknowledge. We're collectively failing too many of our students and our communities. We are stuck in a cycle that enables us to continue that pattern. However, I have found through working with schools that care about their work, through research, and by listening to students, that there is hope. Educational research, proven practices in organizational management, and a commitment to real outcomes for students provide what we need to set a mission and build the capacity of all involved.

Hamster Wheel is a tool for change. It speaks to the urgent need for schools to ask and answer hard questions. It takes a comprehensive look at the data and provides schools with the mettle to refine their mission, develop strong leaders, focus on their own data, and build a community that succeeds for students and faculty alike. The study guide at the end of the book is intended to help thoughtful faculties, educators, and those who work with them ask and answer the hard questions that must be wrestled with if the goals of our intended reforms are going to be met.

Join me and a "Noah's Ark" of characters as we confront the struggles surrounding high school reform and the all-too-present set of low expectations and acceptance of the status quo evidenced in too many of our schools. With metaphors, humor, wit, and true stories from the field, we will take a sobering look at America's high schools. Backed by research and proven best practices we will uncover the truths of the hamster wheel and, more important, how to get off it!

—Grace Sammon
Silver Spring, Maryland

Acknowledgments

In any work that grows from 18 years of being "on the road" with schools, there are many people to thank. Reaching back, I must acknowledge Howard Brown, Cynthia Bell, Zavolia Willis, John Stone, and the D.C. public school system. They had the faith in me to let me help them create the first small learning communities in Washington, D.C. We shared a journey that brought national recognition to a failing school and helped create a movement that took hold in D.C. and inspired a PBS documentary.

Over the course of time, I have had the great privilege of working in such urban centers as Atlanta, Georgia; Baltimore, Maryland; Camden and Newark, New Jersey; Detroit and Muskegon, Michigan; Houston, Texas; Lawrence, Massachusetts; New Orleans, Louisiana; and Philadelphia, Pennsylvania. The lessons learned in these, our most challenged schools, have given me the deepest appreciation for the needs of our youth and the challenges faced by educators. "Urban ring," suburban, and rural schools such as those found in Thornton Township Public Schools just outside Chicago; Salina, Kansas; Newberg and Warwick Valley, New York; Putnam City, Tulsa, and Yukon, Oklahoma; Jordan and Layton, Utah; and Sumner, Washington, face many of the same challenges as their more urban neighbors. They also wrestle with changing demographics, state mandates, and a commitment to continuous improvement. They, too, have invited me on their journey, and we learned how to adapt what we knew to their needs. The wonderful Bureau of Indian Affairs school in Ft. Wingate, New Mexico, helped me to understand the importance of culture in the reform process, the meaning of "small," and the power of a good mission statement. The educators from the Louisiana State Department of Education and from the wonderful bayou schools of LaFourch and Iberia shared candor, culture, and commitment in ways from which I have greatly benefited. The principals, noted in the dedication, from South Grand Prairie, Texas; Hahnville, Louisiana; and Junction

City, Kansas, have dedicated their lives to taking risks and reaping positive results for their schools. Their inclusion of me in their work has been an extraordinary privilege, a humbling experience, and a great reminder of the courage it takes to do this work well. To each of the individuals in these systems I owe my thanks for all I learned from you. I hope that the lessons learned together have helped sustain your work.

To my colleagues at the U.S. Department of Treasury, U.S. Department of Defense, U.S. Navy, and U.S. Department of Health and Human Services, as well as Covenant House–Washington, your commitment to education, and your including me as your support, helped us place the need for school reform and services for children in a community context.

To my colleagues at Johns Hopkins University's Talent Development High Schools, SREB's High Schools That Work, and The Education Alliance at Brown University, it has been a privilege to both serve and support your efforts. And to those at the National Career Academy Coalition, I would not have made this journey without our shared experience.

To the many who have inspired this work as authors, I hope I give your work the credit it deserves and the appropriate credits throughout this book.

There are also those who gave me the encouragement and inspiration to go to print with a tough message on school failure while they urged that I couple it with strategies for success. To Trish McNeil, for believing in me and the work and for the countless conversations and e-mails; to Steve Klink, who got excited by "the wheel" concept and provided a wonderful haven for writing; to Cynthia Conwell and Josephine Rice, outstandingly committed educators of excellence—they were the first readers and said they thought I had it right; and to Billie Donegan, who is first and foremost a teacher from whom I continue to learn. Tonia Essig has for 14 years stayed the course and risen to the challenges of the schools we serve and to those of supporting my work. She has served as an invaluable researcher and resource on this book. To Lizzie Brenkus at Corwin who encouraged my questioning and involvement and cheered me on. I owe each of them my deepest gratitude.

At the end of the day, there are those who simply believe in me. To all the Sammons, Sharon Barrett, Nora Miller, Debbie Muller, Rosemary Byrne, PPA, and T, who always stand by me. Thank you for many years of listening, fun, friendship, and shared journeys. To my dad, Bob Sammon, who, at 87, is my best cheerleader. He is always my first and best editor—MS Word Review mode and all! His presence, and my mother's, is dearly felt in all that I do. This is a great source of inspiration, joy, and solace.

To my fabulous son, B, standard-bearer exemplar. He challenges me with love and shares a journey of the heart. And to my wonderful daughter Kate, full of brilliance and creativity, who, in the simple act of wanting her mom back, gave me the courage to jump off the wheel.

Corwin Press gratefully acknowledges the contributions of the following individuals:

Sharon E. Barrett, Former Director
Office of Minority and Women's Health, Bureau of Primary Health Care
United States Department of Health and Human Services, Rockville, MD

Chuck Bonner, Assistant Principal
Great Valley High School, Malvern, PA

Gwen Gross, Superintendent
Manhattan Beach Unified School District, Manhattan Beach, CA

Melba Kennedy, Assistant Administrator
Louisiana State Board of Elementary and Secondary Education
Louisiana Department of Education, Baton Rouge, LA

About the Author

Grace Sammon, president and founder of GMS Partners, Inc., is an educator, school reformer, consultant, "coach," speaker, and internationally recognized author. Sammon has spent nearly 20 years working in one of the United States' toughest institutions, the American high school. She has inspired change in schools, districts, and government organizations nationally through her upbeat advice and sound, practical recommendations.

GMS Partners, Inc., is an educational consulting firm dedicated to enhancing school communities through a focused effort on vision, alignment of resources, planning, coaching, professional development, and a commitment to continuous improvement. Under Ms. Sammon's leadership, GMS Partners, Inc., has worked in 32 states across the nation with a focus on whole-school reform. She is the president of the Business Institute for Educators and the co-founding director of the National Career Academy Coalition (NCAC). Her clients include schools and school systems at the district and state level, non-profits, and the U.S. Departments of Defense, Education, Health and Human Services, and Navy.

Ms. Sammon has authored the book and CD-ROM Tool Kit *Creating and Sustaining Small Learning Communities: A Practitioner's Guide to Career Academies and Other Small Learning Communities*, eight manuals on school-to-career transition, and articles on organizational change, school partnerships, and staff development. She has created "Metro MANIA: The Great Train Ride Through Washington," a board and street experience game to facilitate student use of public transportation while they gain an appreciation for the employment and cultural offerings of the nation's capital. She has also authored five integrated curricular pieces for use in middle schools and a teen pregnancy prevention curriculum and training manual.

She earned her Master's Degree in Education at The Catholic University of America. She has worked in higher education administration for 10 years and has served as an adjunct university professor and a long-term substitute teacher. Her professional notes include listings in *Who's Who in American Education* and being named Outstanding Business Person of the Year by Future Business Leaders of America. In the spring of 1996, she was appointed to the U.S. Secretary of Defense's Joint Civilian Orientation Council.

To the remarkable administrators, principals,
teachers, educators, and students who are striving to improve
their schools and are kind enough to bring me along for the journey.

To the memory of students
Naytero Kop-Moyo Ormond, Kevin Brown, and Josh Shulman.
Each of you continue to remind me what this work is really about.

For principals extraordinaire Barbara Fuselier,
Greg Springston, and the late Kim Brown. Each taught me,
in his or her own way, the wisdom of thoughtfulness and courage.

**CORWIN
PRESS**

The Corwin Press logo—a raven striding across an open book—represents the union of courage and learning. Corwin Press is committed to improving education for all learners by publishing books and other professional development resources for those serving the field of PreK–12 education. By providing practical, hands-on materials, Corwin Press continues to carry out the promise of its motto: **"Helping Educators Do Their Work Better."**

CHAPTER ONE

The Battle Begins

> We trained hard . . . but it seemed every time we were beginning to form up into teams we were reorganized. I was to learn later in life that we tend to meet any situation by reorganizing, and what a wonderful method it can be to create the illusion of progress while producing confusion, inefficiency, and demoralization.
>
> —*Gaius Petronious (cited in Fullan, 2001, p. 43)*

Welcome to the world of educational reform. For almost 20 years I have been working in one of America's toughest institutions, our public high schools. It took nearly 17 of those years before I was struck with an image to match the sentiment of Gaius Petronious, that of being on a "hamster wheel," running in place, being accepting of a status quo, with little expectation for success and even less of a commitment to continuous growth and improvement.

As we will see shortly, for more than two decades America's schools have been asked to change, to reform themselves. From this paragraph onward, every time you read the word "change," or "reform," or "redesign," read it not as change for change's sake but as taking the opportunity to continuously improve. The words of Gaius Petronious, spoken nearly 2,000 years ago, could easily serve as the snapshot that captures the never-ending cycle of stabs at improving high schools. This is a book that asks you to break with the illusion of progress and make a commitment to a process of reform that leads to effective practices in teaching and learning. It won't happen over night; ask Gaius Petronious.

Hamster Wheel is a tool for change. It provides a rich mix of real-life stories from the field coupled with solid educational research on schools and effective organizational change strategies. The data speak to the urgent need for schools to ask and answer hard questions. Through the remainder of this book, we'll take a look at the body of research on reform and provide schools with the mettle to refine their mission, develop strong leaders, focus on their own data, and build a community that succeeds for students and faculty alike.

Looking back at the relationship I had with my very first high school system client, the District of Columbia Public Schools, I suppose that the writing of this book began there. As a beginning consultant, I was hired to help create the first "career academy" at Anacostia Senior High School. The Anacostia community of southeast D.C. had a proud tradition of civic leadership, as demonstrated by men like Fredrick Douglass; an ugly current-day counterbalance image as the most crime-ridden section of the nation's capital; and a high school that was failing.

In 1990, I knew little about matters of urban failing schools and how they are affected by the broader context of legislation, socioeconomics, race, culture, and a social climate that expected that the children enrolled in *this* high school, and indeed in most urban systems, would fail. Couple this inexperience with the fact that I actually didn't know what a "career academy" was, and it is amazing that I was hired. Yet, "the white girl," as I was often called, was hired for her successful history of developing teacher training programs, developing strong partnerships for school systems, and for having a stubborn belief that *all* students deserved a high quality education. When I was hired I committed to a quest that continues to this day. How do we create and sustain not just a program but also an environment where there is in place a shared set of high standards, beliefs, policies, practices, and automatic responses that creates a *school culture* that reaps real rewards for *all* students?

The Anacostia adventure was one I took along with a small group of innovative educators. Our challenge was great. We had to change plummeting graduation rates (approximately 19%, if you looked at 9th through 12th-grade transition), high absenteeism, and poor postsecondary performance for the high school's students. Through countless "after church lets out" Sunday meetings and late afternoons at the school, we created the Public Service Academy. I had the extraordinary privilege of working with Howard Brown, Telford Anderson, James Dickens, Eddie Mims, Virginia Moore, John Stone, Sue Thomas, and Zavolia Willis. We imagined; we argued; we planned; we fought; we studied; we experimented; we failed; we watched our data; and we never questioned "the union contract." As we grew both more confident and more aware of our skill gaps, we engaged university and government partners in our work. We were each our own worst enemies and each other's greatest supporters. We would give our lives for the program and its initial 41 students. We absolutely believed that we could, *and should*, do absolutely everything in our power to deliver a high-outcomes education for the students for whom we had such high expectations. Yet, I am embarrassed to say that our "high expectation" in those first years was simply that the students would stay in school and graduate.

We knew it wouldn't be easy. It was an uphill battle against the low expectations so many had for "*those* Anacostia students." It was a battle against the status quo of failed reforms, of the rotation of principals and superintendents, and of mid-course changes in funding streams. It was a battle to learn all we needed to learn to create a "career academy." The only available examples were in Pennsylvania and California, and the studies at that time weren't showing us that these were proven programs, just promising ones.

We also had to fight the jealousy of the "non-academy" teachers. Ours was a "pocket" or stand-alone program. This was before the days of "wall-to-wall" whole-school reform. "School as usual" was still the norm for the majority of the Anacostia student body. We realized that when the non-academy teachers saw the gains in attendance and positive student behaviors, they perceived our students as "specially selected." They were jealous of the increased business partnerships and the opportunities our students had through job shadowing. Being in Washington, D.C., we worked hard at incorporating these important work-based opportunities into the curriculum to add relevance to our instruction and to provide an opportunity for our students to see themselves in multiple work venues. Not many students can talk about tap dancing with Vice President Al Gore in his office; or about having lunch in the White House, just under the Oval Office, with Thurgood "Goody" Marshall, Jr.; or about watching tiger surgery at the National Zoo; or about meeting with Mayor Marion Barry. Our students did! Other teachers questioned us as we worked as a team. This was something unprecedented in the late 20th century and is still something only hoped for in most American high schools. Our task included both battling and engaging our own community. We had to get the message out to our own faculty that the student selection was indeed random. The kids were changing because of how we treated them! Our basic curriculum approach hadn't changed; our expectations and how we dealt with students and their families did. We now realized that it would take a team approach, and the broader community, to help us raise these children into the adults they themselves dreamed of being, even if we were uncertain of all the outcomes.

We were constantly battling our own fatigue. We were also battling a dearth of resources. Our students came to us with so many challenges. Of our initial class of 41, I believe only two students read at grade level. All could qualify for free and reduced lunch. Some of our students came to us from the dire circumstances of homelessness and violence. Still others came from the more traditional, solid, two-parent working families. By student report, their greatest need was for grief counseling. Too many of their friends and relatives fell victim to the violence of the streets each week. The students voiced hopes for five years after high school when they imagined themselves doctors, or vets, or government workers. More commonly, they hoped simply to be alive. We nurtured their positive aspirations, knowing that if they could not see their future they risked not having one. We needed to find clothes, food, and social services for these students. We provided "college buddies" through the unfailing support of Dr. Kathy Newcomer at George Washington University's School of Public Policy and Public Administration. We had to do what English teacher Sue Thomas suggested: "provide the services that we can't count on the home doing any more."

It was a mammoth undertaking to pioneer working in teams, engaging the guidance department, marshalling community resources, and focusing on what we taught and how we taught it. In an attempt to better understand the student experience, there was the horrific weekend when we all took the SAT exam along with them—and subsequently had to deal with our results.

At one point, I wanted to walk away. The challenge was too great. We weren't making the progress I thought we should. And, quite frankly, the battles were too hard. A school official took me aside and said, "Progress doesn't matter. Honesty, integrity, and merit don't matter. What matters is taking the money and getting at least at the surface of the job." With that attitude, I knew we were in trouble. There were some among us who believed the status quo was acceptable, that, indeed, it could not be changed. They believed that somehow it would be acceptable if we just looked like we were trying, or worse, that the system would be forgiving if we failed.

We were at what Malcolm Gladwell in his book *The Tipping Point* (2002) would call, well, a tipping point. We wanted to believe that we could create the "magic moment when an idea, trend, or social behavior crosses a threshold, tips, and spreads like wildfire." We were either going to tread water or we were going to push the envelope and be about success for children. I put a large poster from the Computer Curriculum Corporation over my desk that said, simply, "Expect great things!" It represented a commitment to what we were trying to accomplish for *all* students.

Luckily, there was some groundswell of support for our work at Anacostia, and the student data we were closely monitoring proved we were making important gains. We stayed the course. Four years later, we had a 93% graduation rate, which we were able to maintain for several years. Most of the students went on to college. Many had scholarships, some with money from a fund established by our advisory board chairman, John Stone. We were able to document that five years after their graduation, 84% of the students we located were either in college, at work, or dually engaged. That success caught the attention of Hedrick Smith and resulted in the PBS documentary "Across the River." It brought national attention to the Public Service Academy and the many rich and positive aspects of life in this beleaguered Anacostia community. We were also "studied" under the microscope of the nationally recognized Manpower Demonstration Research Corporation's (MDRC) research project on career academies. Based on our work, the entire Anacostia High School went "wall-to-wall," with every student in an academy beginning in September, 1996. In subsequent years, we were asked to replicate the Anacostia project at five other D.C. schools and at one of their adult education centers. We were studied, at Phelps High School, under the RAND Corporation's academy study with additional positive results (Elliot, Gilroy, & Hanser, 2002). The momentum for school reform—the focus on high school improvement—was growing nationally, and the lessons learned from the work of these dedicated teachers and administrators was adding valuable research to the development of reform. The work continues in D.C. today. In mid-2004, Washington, D.C. received a Federal Small Learning Community grant with the goal of bringing similar success to all district schools.

All these years later, the lessons learned at Anacostia are the ones that still have the greatest impact for the direction of my work. Every school and district has "those" kids, and every school and school district can do better for *all* kids. It is hard, but it isn't rocket science. In my first book, *Creating and Sustaining Small Learning Communities* (2000), I was able to couple the lessons learned from Anacostia with those from other schools to create a step-by-step guide for schools on how to look at, develop, and evaluate the creation of smaller learning communities. It was naïve to think that it would be a terminal work. The pace of high school reform is unrelenting; much has changed since I published that book. We understand that change is not an event but a process. We know a lot about adherence to data and developing structures in tandem with a focus on instruction. We know more about vision, mission, planning, and leadership. We see the impact of No Child Left Behind (NCLB) and of severe cuts in educational programs that will challenge reform efforts. We know now that effective reform is definitely not about creating or implementing a program. We know that smaller learning communities, career academies, advocacy or advisory programs, or extra help academic supports, when implemented as stand-alone programs operating in a vacuum of the larger picture of school reform, will not reap the rewards of a systemic approach. Those of us deeply involved in this work know that only a systemic overhaul of the American high school will increase teacher effectiveness and academic outcomes for *all* students.

In the broadest sense, we are talking about an overhaul that will create good high schools for all students. In my organization, GMS Partners, Inc., creating a good high school means focusing on *just* five things: data and mission management; creating personalized communities for teaching and learning; having a laser-like focus on a high standards curriculum; developing strong parent, community, and postsecondary partnerships; and creating a climate for success.

A climate for success demands

- A clear mission and vision,
- Achievable and aligned school plans and resources,
- Appropriate professional development,
- Truly shared and empowered leadership,
- A commitment to continuous improvement, and
- A climate of respect for school staff and students alike.

Creating these schools requires hard work and significant change. While I would like to believe that the change process can be a step-by-step linear one, it is in fact quite messy. To build from Michael Fullan's work, there is no easy way to push through either the social-psychological fear of change experienced by educators or the lack of technical know-how or skills to make the change work (Fullan, 2003, p. 41).

The change, or high school reform movement, is being fueled by some pretty big players. The U.S. Department of Education (USED) is revising one of its largest high school and postsecondary programs, the Carl Perkins Act, and it is forging new partnerships with the U.S. Department of Labor in an effort to both improve educational options for students and improve the workforce of the future. In addition, USED has been channeling approximately $420 million per year, over the course of five years, into the Smaller Learning Community Program. National funders such as the Annenberg and Carnegie Foundations are pumping millions of dollars into reforms in key places such as Atlanta, Boston, Chattanooga, Chicago, Detroit, Houston, Los Angeles, New York City, Philadelphia, Salt Lake City, and San Francisco. Local funders are also deeply committed to a change process. In Baltimore City alone, local funders contributed more than $10 million for the benefit of just nine neighborhood high schools. Of course, the big gorilla in the room when it comes to funding high school reform is the Bill and Melinda Gates Foundation, which, by July 2005, had contributed more than $2 billion to education, of which $700,000 had gone directly to high schools. It's not just a question of the funding. NCLB, regardless of how it may be amended, will only demand an increase in high-stakes testing and student outcomes before students will be allowed to graduate.

Increasingly we are seeing books, conferences, Web sites, and articles that focus on the state of today's high schools. The focus began under U.S. Education Secretary Terrell Bell with the National Commission on Excellence in Education and its now-famous report, *A Nation at Risk* (1983). The report did not shy away from describing the poor performance of American students in international comparisons and the continued gaps between poor and minority students and white students. It demanded that all students receive a rigorous academic curriculum. Ever since, our educational system has been involved in a critical transformation. The dialogue continued in the National Association of Secondary School Principals' (NASSP) 1996 report, *Breaking Ranks,* which outlined the need for high schools to be learning communities that provide effective transition into postsecondary learning and work. The report advised high schools to support students in their personal development and "unabashedly advocate for young people." In spring, 2004, NASSP released *Breaking Ranks II,* which adds even more to what we know and should be able to do for students in our schools. This report focuses on three core areas: sowing the seeds for change through collaborative leadership, professional learning communities, and the strategic use of data; personalizing the school environment; and making learning personal through the lens of curriculum, instruction, and assessment (NASSP, 2004, p. xi).

There are many excellent books and Web resources on effective schools and on effective organizations. Most of the literature pays homage to the craft of teaching and the dedication of teachers. Yet, as educators we are being asked to reinvent our industry and ourselves. All of these resources call for a reform of the educational process, as do our central administration buildings and federal mandates. Depending on which educational reform camp you belong to, this means that the American high school needs to undergo reform, reinvention, redesign, conversion, reconfiguration, transformation, or, as one Texas educator noted, *obliteration*. No matter which moniker you use, there seems to be at least one consensus: schools, as they currently exist, need to change.

But why change, and to what?

Like many of you, I have, over the course of 18 years of working in high schools, seen reform initiatives come and go. I have witnessed educators meet with varying degrees of success and have participated in national debates focusing on the status of the American high school. At no time in the history of education have the stakes been raised so high concerning the education of all of America's children. Educators at the federal, state, district, school, and classroom level, as well as researchers, technical assistance providers, and community groups, are all grappling with how to make their reform initiatives work. However, the beliefs, policies, and practices—the culture of schools, and particularly that of high schools—have not helped schools meet with success. Some educators are waiting so that they can, as one teacher in Louisiana said to me, "just get back to the business of teaching." The problem with that statement is that the business of teaching has changed. Teaching is not about going to our classroom and mastering just our subject matter. It is about addressing the needs of the whole child, working in collaboration with our colleagues, and committing to our own continuous improvement at the craft we call teaching. We can no longer work in the isolation of our classrooms or in isolation from a changing world culture and the reforms it requires. "Isolation," as former New York City District 2 Superintendent Tony Alvarado states, "is the enemy of improvement" (cited in Silva & Mackin, 2002, p. xi). Too many of us are clinging to a paradigm that can no longer exist. The research bears out that our students are not excelling and the reforms are meeting with only mixed success. Too often, the culture of schools has educators engaged in a cycle of reforms that keeps them running without making the progress the reforms seek to attain.

Tony Wagner, in *Making the Grade: Reinventing America's Schools* (2003), calls to the front of the education dialogue key questions regarding the structures of schools meeting the needs of today's students. As we will see in Chapter 3, he is absolutely committed to asking and answering the hard questions that make for successful schools. He eloquently pushes the envelope on a debate about creating a good high school and the leadership that reinvention takes. He also states, however, that the schools in America have not failed. Data proves we are actually educating more students than ever before. Looking at one indicator, we see the math SAT has recently reported the highest national scores in 30 years. "Schools aren't failing," states Wagner; indeed, "schools haven't really changed— for the better or the worse. The world has." Wagner finds that drawing a distinction between school failure and schools that are not meeting their mission because they have become obsolete is a critical difference that helps educators understand the magnitude and nature of the challenge (Wagner, 2003, p. 136). Stanford's Linda Darling-Hammond pushes the need for change from a different perspective in *The Right to Learn: A Blueprint for Creating Schools that Work* (1997). She puts forward that

> in the eyes of most educators, parents, employers, and students, our educational system is failing. Rigid and bureaucratic, it was never designed to teach all children effectively, to teach learners in all their varieties, to attend to each child's particular mix of aptitudes and barriers to learning. (p. 25)

In Darling-Hammond's view, we have solid research that says we are lagging as a nation.

> Students in high-achieving states like Iowa, Minnesota, and North Dakota do as well in mathematics as those in high scoring countries like Korea and Japan, while students in low-achieving states like Alabama, Louisiana, and Mississippi do far worse, ranking at the bottom of the distribution. (p. 25)

The changing demographics of society and a changed economic climate are placing new demands on the educational system.

Without laying blame on anyone's doorstep, it is clear that we are losing ground. In the middle of the 20th century, approximately 20% of all U.S. jobs required training beyond high school. As we settle into the 21st century, high school dropouts have only a 33% chance of even finding work. If they do find employment, they will earn less than half of what they would have earned in 1968. Studies show that as many as 60% of employers and university professors believe that high school graduates do not have the requisite skills to compete and contribute effectively in the job or education arenas. We are failing too many of our students.

Thomas Toch summarizes the history of the American high school and the challenge our educational system and students face in his *High Schools on a Human Scale: How Small Schools Can Transform American Education* (2003). He states,

- The basic blueprint for high schools hasn't changed since the rise of the comprehensive high school nearly a century ago. (p. 1)
- The comprehensive high schools were created to do something quite different from what we want and need high schools to do today. (p. 1)
- The utilitarian system . . . served the purpose of the nation's industrial economy. High schools served as sorting machines, preparing students very differently for roles in the workplace. (p. 3)
- The new economy requires a new and different priority: that nearly every student be educated well enough to enter college. (p. 5)
- The anonymity that pervades many public high schools saps students' motivation to learn and teachers' motivation to teach. (p. 7)
- For many students, large comprehensive high schools are joyless, uninspiring places. (p. 10)
- For a majority of students, particularly African American and Hispanic students and those from disadvantaged families, a large, comprehensive high school is an educational dead end, where low expectations and tracking swell enrollment in [the less demanding academic] courses. (p. 9)

Other researchers support Toch's work and point to high schools as bleak and joyless places for students. A recent *USA Today* "Snapshots" titled "School Day Doldrums" reported that for 11% of students between 8 and 18, every day in school is a bad day (Bryant & Liu, 2003).

Given the growing focus on high schools, some will believe we are in an education crisis; others will say we simply need to tweak a few things for *some* students. But regardless of the perceived needed level of change, we are losing far too many of our students to the nation's "drop out factories" (Balfanz & Legters, 2004, p. 5), and we are able to document far too many students, even in our "high-performing schools," as disengaged from their learning and their futures. The numbers are too high, on both counts, to allow America to remain competitive in a global economy. And they are too high, I believe, to allow any of us a good night's sleep, as we will see in Chapter 2. This unsettling reality challenges educators, the overwhelming majority of whom entered the profession out of a commitment to children's learning.

Given this reality, you might think we need to determine anew what makes a good high school; however, the practitioners and researchers have already done it. We'll delve into the details later in this book. For now, we have a significant body of knowledge that says the good high school is

- Small, or provides the sense of small,
- Committed to high academic expectations for *every* student,
- Personalized, where students are known well by adults,
- Committed to ongoing study and collaboration in the instructional practice of the educators and administrators,
- Focused on instruction and has multiple forms of assessment,
- Providing extra help and advisory support for students,
- Centered on a culture where everyone's voice, even the students', is heard and respected,
- Working under a thoughtful plan that aligns improvement and reform efforts, and
- Seriously committed to continuous improvement regardless of how high they already score on their state's test.

I contend that while ongoing research is critical to our success with schools, we already have all the books, articles, and basic research that tells us what we should be doing for schools. Certainly, there is the broad national context of politics and community practice that impacts this work, but the core question is, "If we know what it is we are trying to create, why do we find school reform such a difficult and onerous process, and why are we not attaining the measurable and sustained goals that we set?" It is not for lack of a skilled faculty. I believe we have competent educators. It is not, as we may wish to believe, a crisis of finances. Despite what some may say, the lack of resources is rarely specifically financial. We are not underfunded in American education; indeed, compared to Germany, France, Japan, Belgium, and the United Kingdom, the United States spends, on average, 45% more per pupil on education.

My hypothesis is simple: we have neither recognized that the schools we have created can no longer serve the needs of all students nor have we made a commitment to build the capacity of our educators to make the necessary changes in the schools to meet with success. Educators are steeped in a culture that has not, traditionally, required innovation or change. Adults alive today were bred in an educational tradition that was designed to allow for the masses to take their places in an economy and culture that no longer exist. We work in a culture that has allowed isolationism. We have not demanded attention to student data. We have not paid attention to results for all students. We have not kept pace with a changing society, and we have not had the courage to hold each other accountable for student and school success. In education, and in many other industries, we have become so focused on the multiple tasks of our work, the amount that is expected of us, the demands of our families and our society, and the pace of our lives that we have not stopped to take stock of whether we are actually accomplishing *the mission* of our organizations.

It is not the knowing what to create that stymies us, it is the knowing how. Frederick Hess, director of Education Policy Studies at the American Enterprise Institute, recently wrote that

> the crisis is that the performance we deemed adequate 50 years ago is neither tolerable nor defensible today. The crisis is that too few of our schools are excellent, so many are mediocre, and yet, we, the adults responsible, are content to tinker and theorize. (Hess, 2004, p. 2)

Hess's reality hit home for me in the spring of 2003.

I had grown a lot as a school reformer since my Anacostia days. I'd written *Creating and Sustaining Small Learning Communities,* become a "national speaker," created a national nonprofit organization focused on career academies, and published articles. I continued to work at some of the nation's toughest schools and some wonderful ones—and, sometimes, they were both at once. I had already worked in more than 30 states in urban, suburban, and rural communities and on Native American lands. I had begun to work not only at the school level but also at the district, state, and federal levels of education. I learned as much from schools as I brought to the table. The level of risk, creativity, and commitment that district and school administrators, as well as classroom teachers, voiced for reform work always impressed me. I had had the great opportunities to work with Johns Hopkins University's Talent Development High Schools, the Small Schools Workshop, and the Education Alliance at Brown University, as well as the Southern Regional Education Board's High Schools That Work. GMS Partners, my company, now had a team of seven qualified educators and reformers who made our successes possible. We had learned the lessons of sensitivity to culture and the process of organizational change. We had mastered, as close as anyone can, how to identify, be sensitive to, and be inclusive of negotiated agreements and union contracts. We had developed protocols, workshops, and tools. We had refined our coaching style. We knew that real change needs to be supported from "the top" and grown in the school with the principal and in each classroom. We understood that a good principal mattered—a lot—but nothing outweighed a dedicated group of good teachers. So, imagine my surprise one lovely spring evening in 2003.

I sat in a meeting in Maryland with a dedicated and committed school improvement team. In my opinion, that school had won the prize. They had a new school, a new visionary principal, committed business and postsecondary partners, involved parents, a rich balance of "seasoned" and new faculty, the time and support to meet each week, and they had inherited a student body of just 700 students. In addition, they had received multiple grants from the Gates Foundation, local sponsors, and the Federal Smaller Learning Community program. They had a rigorous mission statement, a supportive superintendent, and a High School Steering Committee.

In my role as technical assistant, or TA provider, it was my job to meet with the group each week as we added depth to a design that required us to create a school that was committed to just three things:

- Small supportive structures,
- Academic rigor, and
- Effective leadership and instruction.

We met tirelessly for five weeks from 3:00 until 6:00 P.M. We worked hard. We imagined; we argued; we planned; we fought; we studied. (Sound familiar?) We had minutes of our meetings, printed agendas, handouts, e-mails, a library of resources, a paid facilitator, and "the white girl" (as I was still called). We had the really nice, and all-important, binder for our "School Reform Committee," and, most important, we had *snacks*.

In week five, however, I realized *we had actually also made no progress*. We continued to rehash old decisions; we brought new folks up-to-date; and we re-thought, re-discussed, and re-fought old battles. We fretted about football teams and chorus more than we ever did about the students' needs and quality of instruction. We had not gotten to the important questions of structures, rigor, or leadership. We had not gotten to the deeper discussions needed about academic achievement, professional community, and data-driven decisions.

I had the disquieting sense that everyone was actually quite satisfied with the "progress" we were making. Indeed, if I had stopped to do a survey, I am sure that the participants would have rated our reform process "successful." After all, we had agendas, and minutes, *and binders*, *and snacks*. We were operating as we always operated. Indeed, we were in the process of simply creating a smaller version of the larger school of which we were once a part. If surveyed, folks would have politely smiled and nodded that we were on the right road. And in their assent they would have provided support for the silent voice that so often kills reform.

In an epiphany I had the blazing image of a hamster on a wheel. You know, those adorable little animals that spend their lives running endlessly on their exercise wheels, ultimately going nowhere. In that moment, I knew we were on our own hamster wheel. We were running in place; we were not on a road to success. If I closed my eyes I could almost hear the soft, squeaky, incessant *"whirr, whirr, whirr"* of the wheel spinning. What was worse for me was that I knew I no longer had any expectation that we would move forward. I had indeed just hopped right up on the wheel with this team. *Whirr! Whirr! Whirr!*

The school in Maryland was not an isolated instance. Let me provide a snapshot of my more challenging experiences with high schools:

- A principal called me from Florida and said she heard that I was an expert in school reform. She said that she needed help with that. When I asked what her data was telling her, what she believed we should be concentrating on, and what the ultimate result of her reform would be, her response was, "I am not sure. I was told I had to do school reform so I have to reform this school. What can you do to make that happen?"
- A school in Louisiana called. They were in the second year of an implementation grant. They were hoping that I could come down and help them *begin planning*. They hadn't been ready to do the work before.
- I called a school that I was working with in Michigan because I had heard that a student had shot himself in the building that day. The assistant principal was puzzled by my call. She indicated he had *"just* been playing with the gun *in his pocket"* and it had gone off, injuring his leg. For this school, this was routine.
- A colleague from a large midwestern city called to bemoan district strategy. It was the fourth week of school. Tomorrow was to be the all-important "count day," the day that numbers are registered for school populations and funding cycles. The city was more than 25,000 down in their count. None of the special education children had yet received bus transportation for the year, and thus they had already missed four weeks of school. In an attempt to ensure attendance on count day, ice cream coupons were promised to all students, and buses were hired for special education students; however, parents had not yet been notified of the bus schedule.
- One of my clients was about to turn back $400,000 in unspent funds to the grantor without so much as an inquiry regarding extending the work.

- A school system in Louisiana reported that it now had all of its students in smaller learning communities because they had changed their bell schedule to a block schedule.
- In Detroit, four out of ten of the principals we worked with buried students during a one-week period of cross-city violence.
- In a suburb of New York City, a school working toward the creation of a 9th grade voted it down when one teacher did not want to move her classroom.
- In an Oklahoma school, the students were supporting 90-minute block scheduling because their teachers were "so efficient that they could still teach everything needed in 45 minutes; then they, the students, had another 45 to study or do homework."
- In the central part of the country, a faculty was complacent about the fact that they had 460 freshman and only 169 seniors. They were eager to blame the loss of students on mobility, but no one there could cite the mobility rate.
- During a late-winter school observation in the south, I saw a student shrinking, almost literally, into a wall and another in the same class sound asleep. When I questioned what was going on the teacher mentioned that those two students had indicated back in the fall that they would be dropping out on their 16th birthdays in the spring, so she saw no reason to continue to work with them.
- A high-performing school in Iowa contacted me to discuss increasing personalization for their students. After conducting a community survey, they had determined that most parents would be satisfied if "more students have the opportunity to become homecoming queen."
- A school in the south contacted me, excited that they had, at last, chosen a theme for their first smaller learning community. "We've decided on a jewelry academy!" (With my sometimes-odd sense of humor, I thought, "Well, the homecoming queens in Iowa would think that was a good idea.") What I said, of course, was "Have you considered how such a program would engage all students to high standards, build relevancy, and transition students to a wide and successful range of postsecondary experiences?"

Whirr! Whirr! Whirr!

I have been spending a lot of time observing, reflecting, prodding, and studying what I now call the "hamster wheel phenomenon." Sadly, it seems to resonate with many of the schools with which I work and the organizations that I have studied. I realize, as they do, that many of our best-intended and hard working schools are still fighting the battles we fought at Anacostia, but now the stakes are even higher. Educators are still trying, but they are not seeing the gains their state mandates, mission statements, and hearts tell them they should. Since you've picked up this book, I have to believe that you may have had similar experiences and that you believe, at least in part, that we are not winning the battle for effective systemic reform. I still have that "Expect Great Things!" poster hanging in my office. Perhaps it was Pollyanna-ish to expect the attitude that it helped engender in me to last, but for 17 of my 18 years working in schools, it worked.

I am hard on teachers, and I am hard on schools because I know we can succeed, and I know how we can get off the wheel! I want our children to be the successful lifelong learners our mission statements say they will be. But, as Mahatma Gandhi said, "The future will depend on what we do in the present." Change and continuous improvement will not happen without a focused approach. Throughout this book, I paint an honest picture of high schools based both on my experience and the national data, yet I worry that you will take offense at my honesty. I worry more that schools will continue to write unattainable plans and orchestrate extensive, disconnected staff development. I worry that educators will continue to go to conferences, read good books and articles, and hire good consultant support but still fail to get to the place where they see reform with results. While the picture I paint is sometimes bleak, it is not one without hope. Through working with schools that care about their work, through research, and by listening to students, I believe we have found a successful focus for reform and redesign. Educational research, proven practices in organizational management, and a commitment to real outcomes for students provide what we need. These factors help us to set a mission and build the capacity of all involved.

As a nation, we are being asked to change our schools. We can no longer, if we ever could, settle for the status quo. The question is "Do we have the courage to do it?" Frederick Hess (2004) states, "*Status quo reformers* believe that the nation's millions of teachers and administrators are already doing the best they can and the only way to improve America's schools is to provide money, expertise, training, and support" (p. 4). In this book, I state that I know what it's like to be there. Thankfully, because of the students and the excellent teachers I have met and worked with, I know there are ways to get off the wheel, but it's still a battle. We know what we want for our schools; however, too often we do not create a climate for success that allows that vision to take hold.

As educators, we are on a shared journey. Welcome to my world! Two hundred days a year on the road working with schools in 32 states; I am entering my 19th year as a reformer. I see educators working hard. Many are running on that wheel. But we can't let them stay there—we cannot leave them alone. Indeed, most do not want to stay there! We must be like Don Quixote who, many thought, battled just windmills. We must battle the status quo and the low expectations so many have for our schools and organizations. We must acknowledge that even we sometimes believe the system is unbeatable. We must fight the temptation to hop on, stay on, or allow others to be on a hamster wheel. I invite you on my journey and that of the schools I have had the great privilege of working with. Together, we will learn to battle and win against the hamster wheel!

> *First they ignore you, then they laugh at you, then they fight you, then you win.*
>
> —Mahatma Gandhi

The Battle Begins

- The terms *change, reform, reinvention, redesign, conversion, reconfiguration, transformation,* or *obliteration* are really all about a commitment to continuous improvement of educational practice that reaps rewards for all students.
- Change is a process, not an event.
- It's not about creating a program but a systemic overhaul of the policies and practices in place in the high school.
- There are five key areas for focus: data-driven management, personalized learning environments, strong curriculum, deep partnerships, and a commitment to a climate for success.
- A climate for success requires a clear mission and vision, achievable and aligned school plans and resources, appropriate professional development, truly shared and empowered leadership, a commitment to continuous improvement, and a climate of respect for school staff and students.
- We must create schools that are
  o Small, or provide the sense of small,
  o Committed to high academic expectations for *every* student,
  o Personalized, where students are known well by adults,
  o Focused on instruction and have multiple forms of assessment,
  o Providing extra help and advisory support for students,
  o Centered on a culture where everyone's voice, even the students', is heard and respected,
  o Working under a thoughtful plan that aligns improvement and reform efforts, and
  o Seriously committed to continuous improvement regardless of how high they already score on their state's test.
- Educational research, proven practices in organizational management, and a commitment to real outcomes for students provide what we need.

CHAPTER TWO

The Skunk Is on the Table

T his is a chapter about honesty.

The world of school reform is often filled with high hopes. It is also far too frequently coupled almost immediately with confusion about competing initiatives, tension, bruised egos, dysfunction, and a sense on the part of educators that they are being victimized and disrespected. While none of those feelings are intended or comfortable, they might be worth the price if we were seeing reforms that resulted in successful changes in school culture and positive outcomes for students. Sadly, we are not.

It's true, we are working very hard, but too many of us, at all levels of educational reform, have failed to build into our reform efforts the commitment, capacity, and accountability measures that are necessary to see sustained gains for schools. This lack of an effective reform strategy has provided teachers with too many good excuses not to change. We have failed to support the teachers and administrators who are ready to make a commitment to true reform. We have failed to focus on effective planning and coherent staff development programs. We fail to hire superintendents, principals, and teachers who can value the positive aspects of reform, sustain them, and bring a new level of inquiry to the study and implementation process of creating a good high school. We continue to fail to value and share our expertise with our colleagues. We fail to align mandates, programs, and consultant work or funding streams with initiatives and the needs we see in our schools. We fail to admit we aren't making gains. We are collectively failing too many of our students and our communities.

I believe we may be stuck in a cycle that enables us to continue that pattern. The cycle is beginning to wear us out. In one east coast community with a new superintendent, the three high school principals reported they are already exhausted just four weeks into the school year as the new superintendent piles on new and competing initiatives. The principals, in turn, demand new and competing efforts from their staffs, and so on. Those of us in similar systems, who still have the energy, are frustrated. And we are getting angry with all we are called to do.

Unless we find ways to commit to change the structures and belief systems that exist in our schools, we are going to stay right where we are. We'll continue to see pockets of excellence for some students, but on a national scale we will not see schools that nurture teachers and students to success. While sometimes less optimistic about the overall reform, I still ardently believe that all teachers want to succeed with their students. I absolutely believe that the people in the schools, those closest to the challenge, are those closest to the solution. I have seen evidence in schools of excellence in teaching coupled with a great passion for and commitment to growth.

Educators are an affable group. Characteristically, we work hard, like people, and like to talk. Most of us even like children. We go out of our way to be nice, to nicely tell his mother "why Johnny can't read." We have a love of learning and we want to share that. We are capable of adapting to changing administrators and changing initiatives. We are used to managing time and juggling priorities. We believe we are doing a good job but that schools in general can improve. We probably don't believe that reform necessarily needs to happen in *our* building, but we are willing to listen—at least until it affects *our own* classroom.

In the focus groups I conduct with teachers, they tell me they are tired. Tired of the cycle of reform, tired of the increased demands, and tired of schools and society not having the resources or willingness to make the hard choices to truly effect improvement. Too many schools engage in an ineffective study process and then choose what one researcher called "the Julie Andrews method of reform"—one in which schools simply implement "a few of their favorite things." Successful schools have a systemic approach that is linked to their mission; they do not choose a few of their favorite things.

I said this was going to be a chapter about honesty. Dr. Phil, of *Oprah* and now with his own significant fame, uses a down-home, tough love statement when he's being honest: he "throws the skunk on the table." The premise is that there are things that need to be talked about; it doesn't matter how much they stink. Ignoring them doesn't help; you have to deal with the skunk. My colleague Billie Donegan and I have found the blatant honesty of the statement so effective that we have purchased as many plush toy skunks as we can find and regularly "award" them to our different clients as they agree to grapple with the tough issues, ask the hard questions, and honestly assess their work.

The first skunk on the table is owning up to your own hamster wheel phenomenon—those times when we are spinning our wheels and not making the progress we need to improve our lives, communities, and schools. We've all been there in a job, in a relationship, in an organization, and, for our purposes, in a school. Reflect for a minute.

Have you ever experienced any or all of the following?

- You are sitting, over and over again, in what Howard Brown from Anacostia used to call "the first meeting." You know, these are the meetings when you are constantly re-deciding what you decided last time and bringing up to speed the people who should have been at the last meeting so that they can help decide all the things the original group of people decided several meetings ago.
- You've attended meetings that didn't need to take place, that took you away from a "mission critical" task. They may have even been good meetings, but they had no clear purpose or outcome. According to author David Cottrell, "the average person spends 250 hours per year in unproductive meetings." (Cottrell, 2002, p. 68)
- You've let creep into your belief system that only some children can learn, only some teachers can teach, and only some schools can succeed.
- You have allowed, or been victim of someone who has allowed, policies and tradition to stifle creativity, or good teaching, or the asking of the essential question about what makes sense for student learning.
- You've participated in a disjointed set of professional development programs that are disconnected from your needs and that provide no follow-up support.
- You've been in your school, organization, or department long enough to feel that you are engaged in what I call "flavor of the month" reforms. You know, "let's try this this month, see if it works (or is forgotten), and then we'll try something else next month, semester, or year."
- You have no funds to do the work you want to further your mission, yet your school or district is about to turn back unspent grant funds.
- You see little or no gain in student outcomes, or no change in the culture of the school to allow student and teacher voices to be respected.

- You think the 1993 Bill Murray movie *Groundhog Day* (in which the main character is forced to continuously relive the worst day of his life until he learns to become a better person) feels remarkably like what you are experiencing in school reform.

Whirr, Whirr, Whirr. Can you hear it?

Does the above list remind you of those addiction surveys you may have seen? You know, the ones that state, "If you checked 'yes' to two of the above statements you may have a problem. If you checked 'yes' to more than two you do have a problem. Seek help immediately!" Indeed, if you identified with the list you may be working in a system that is addicted to operating on a hamster wheel. And, if you are very honest, you may realize that you have, in some way, contributed to that cycle.

If you recognize yourself and your organization above, jot down a few of your own hamster wheel experiences and shout "Amen." We've taken the first step. We are beginning to recognize the problem. We are not laying blame. We are beginning to take schools, as we say we take the children who come to them, "where they are." But like the kids, we need to move our schools to where they need to be. As Tony Wagner states, "no blame, no shame, no excuses" (Wagner, 2003, p. 137).

One of our main challenges in education is that we have failed to study and adapt the rich lessons from organizational change theory that many American and international organizations have espoused successfully. We continue to operate in a nation that allows a great deal of what I term the "disconnect" between policy and practice and a further disconnect between those who set policy and those who have to enact the practice. The disconnections foster a lack of systemic academic achievement for students and an inability to raise the level of effectiveness and respect of the teaching profession. As we will see throughout this book, we suffer from a disconnection between our schools' mission and any number of the following:

- Our hiring practices,
- How we use the resources of data, funding streams, staff, and consultants,
- The planning and delivery of professional development and training,
- How we treat each other as professionals,
- The texts we use in class,
- The way we assess learning,
- The standards movement,

- How we prepare teachers in schools of education,
- How we relate to parents and the postsecondary education, business, and community-based organizations, and
- How we relate to students.

For those willing to work though the process of reform, the disconnects are a breeding ground for frustration. The disconnections, at a minimum, cause inefficiency. At worst, they cause ineffective instructional and operational practice that results in the limited successes seen by some schools. Meanwhile, teachers, administrators, and supporters are working tirelessly, yet some never seem to get off the wheel and see real changes in school culture. The frustration is palpable. I believe we must respect that frustration and the anger that accompanies it and channel it, finally, into effective reform. More and more often I am becoming like Howard Beal in the 1976 movie *Network*; "I am mad as hell, and I don't want to take it anymore." I suspect that what should have happened at the new school start-up meeting in Maryland mentioned in Chapter 1, and what I should have had the wherewithal to help make happen, was that we should have stood up, run to the window like Howard Beal, and shouted. We should have demanded a process that valued our knowledge, skills, and abilities; addressed the gaps we may have in developing and delivering effective instruction; and honored our commitment to education.

There are a lot of us who are angry. A "Google" search using the phrase "I'm mad as hell," quoting *Network's* Howard Beal, turns up 425,000 hits in .41 seconds. People are mad about the state of government, their lawn service, computers, state spending, and their heating and air conditioning units. One family was so angry they created an entire Web page about their most recent family reunion. People are also mad about the state of education. Add the word "education" to the "mad as hell" search, and nearly 95,000 folks are mad about education. As the data I will share in a moment will demonstrate, we should be. Reading the Web sites listed in the search results, we see a theme emerge: people get angry when their expectations are not met.

Many of us entered education because we believed we could transform the lives of our students and the communities in which they live. We entered with high expectations, but increasingly those expectations are being set by state and federal agencies. Now we are told we must operate in a high stakes, high expectations world. We are to embrace as our mantra "all children can learn and all schools can succeed" and, certainly, "no child will be left behind." (Some of my Texas administrators refer to this as "no teacher or principal will be left standing.")

If we really believe in high expectations, shouldn't we be seeing more of our schools succeed in meeting annual yearly progress (AYP)? Shouldn't we be seeing more of our good schools becoming great schools? The data speak clearly. While we are seeing modest gains in elementary and middle schools, we are continuing to fail our high school students. A survey of high school teachers will tell you that their students come to them woefully underprepared to do high school work. A survey of 90,000 students by Indiana University researchers found that students feel less challenged by their work as they progress through high school. Year after year we are losing literally thousands of youth to the rolls of dropouts and drift outs. Recent articles have pointed to as many as one-third of American youth no longer graduating from high school. Those who are staying in school are not succeeding at acceptable levels on state tests, nor taking increased numbers of honors or AP classes, nor going on to colleges at the rates that researchers tell us will be essential if we are to be a world leader in a knowledge-based society.

I simply want schools to succeed.

The way we begin to make this happen is to begin to channel the energy of the teaching population into work that they can and will engage in. I believe educators want to, can, and must engage in

- A meaningful process of creating and developing professional communities where they look at their data and use them effectively,
- Developing plans for their schools that are attainable,
- Refining their skills,
- Succeeding with students,
- Studying together,
- Redefining their profession, and
- Receiving the recognition they deserve for doing well the hardest job in America: nurturing students to succeed as individuals eager to learn more and take their place as contributing citizens of our country.

As I began to research, study, observe, and dissect the reform process and began to develop strategies to help the transformation in school policy and practice take place, I noticed, through my by now admittedly biased lens, that indeed many of us are becoming complacent. While we continue to work hard, I see that in parking lots, teachers' lounges, and central administration offices we are beginning to utter our quiet beliefs that maybe we can't change, and maybe we can't really succeed for *all* students. I see a growing trend toward wanting to wait out the grant cycle, or the principal, or the superintendent. We are awaiting our retirement or someone else's. We are going to our classrooms, perhaps to pursue excellence there, but we are disconnected from the greater reform. I believe that we have been lulled into a belief system of accepting the status quo, of indeed having little expectation that we can make a true difference in the lives of all students.

The Public Education Network recently featured an article by Arnold Fege, Director of Public Engagement for the Public Education Network, titled *Schools Embrace Innovation* (Fege, 2004). It speaks well to the deluge of new ideas, reforms, and innovations facing schools. Fege talks about how in education we are so desperate for improvements that we buy into any innovation that even remotely suggests that test scores will improve. He suggests, and I concur, that schools are suffering from "innovation fatigue." Teachers are tired. Indeed, we are so pressed by often conflicting or unaligned demands that we often don't even realize that we are not succeeding. We are running as fast as we can, with the best of intentions, but we are on a hamster wheel, not a road to success. *Whirr, whirr, whirr.*

State departments of education, districts, school boards, partnering organizations, individual schools, and the individuals in each of these organizations must find the wherewithal to say "no" to what appear to be quick-fix solutions. We must, instead, take the time to develop and adhere to a coherent approach to school improvement that involves not only educational organizations but also the political, business, and community organizations that share the responsibility for developing an educated citizenry.

Here is a skunk on the table. We, as an educational community, don't know where we are.

As I travel around the country working with schools, I have a series of essential questions I explore with audiences and with small school groups. One is to ask if those present know their school, district, or organization's mission statement. As you read this, do you know yours? By heart? No cheating, no looking up at it pasted on the wall of your office or laminated to the back of your school ID. Do you know it? Unless you or your coworkers are very different from the educators I work with, you don't know it. In a room of 400, I would venture to say that perhaps 10 hands hesitantly go up when the mission question is asked. When I then ask if anyone can give me just the gist of his or her mission statement, there is usually a murmur in the room. The audience then collectively laughs when I make up some statement, slurring my words and blurring together, "high expectations and supporting students to be lifelong learners." They fall silent when I ask if anyone can share with me evidence that any element of their mission statement is regularly enacted as a part of their school culture.

In Michigan two years ago, I was walking down the school corridor with an assistant principal responsible for creating small learning communities. The school's mission statement, prominently displayed at the building's front door, was something along the lines of "In this building we respect all learners." The bell rang. Students scurried, or tarried, on their way to class, and the assistant principal went into action. "Hall sweep!" As she began yelling, and chasing, and berating students she also, literally, corralled them behind a pull-down security gate, shouting, "Get back! Get back!" In a sister school in the same district with a similar mission statement, the principal has armed his staff with electronic megaphones. There I witnessed the school's administration place the devices directly against students' ears and shout, "Get to class." In a society where so many of our children have only two options, the educational system or the penal system, how dare their actions be so *disconnected* from their mission statements? For me, these were painful visualizations of what Peggy Silva and Robert A. Mackin speak of in their book *Standards of Mind and Heart: Creating the Good High School.*

> In America's high schools we are experts at stilling the voices of our children. And in doing so, we foster student uninterest and disenchantment with the process of democracy. Next to prisons, high schools are the least democratic institutions in our American society. (Silva & Mackin, 2002, p. 1)

There are days I would set my "expectation bar" for schools as just being places that respect children.

In Silva and Mackin's book they describe the creation of Souhegan High School. In the creation of that school they are given the same gift as the Maryland school I mentioned earlier. They, too, had the opportunity to build a school from the ground up and to envision a new way of operating and delivering instruction. They took the time to ask the essential questions of what should our mission be, and how will we get there. They spent literally days crafting their mission statement. And now at Souhegan every decision, every activity, every job hire, and even the entire freshman seminar course is linked to understanding and evoking that mission.

If we do not have a clear, laser-like focus on what the true mission of our organization is, how are we to make the right choices for student success? How are we going to minimize the disconnects we see in our practice that leads to failure or mixed results for too many of our students and schools?

We must also have a focus on data, or how else will we know whether we have succeeded? If I have been lucky enough to have you in any of my audiences, or if you have worked with me for even the shortest period of time, you know that I am "math challenged." Since I have said this is a chapter of honesty, I suppose I should admit that my own high school guidance counselor identified my lack of skill in this area early. Although I am forever grateful for being placed in business math and for acquiring the related applicable skills I use even to this day, it was not lost on me that I was being placed with low performers for my last required math course, with no expectation that I would succeed, with no suggestions for how I could get extra help, and with no explanation of the possible implications of taking business math versus a higher level of math. I was in 10th grade. A year later, having taken no math courses in the interim, I proved my guidance counselor's expectations were right by scoring the lowest math SAT of anyone I knew. I am embarrassed that in my first book, the one on small learning communities, my entire nod to data is something along the lines of "data are good, use them." That is now all changed. Four years later, there is not a conversation about high school work that does not start with "What data are we looking at and what do they tell us needs to be done?"

In a like manner to my mission statement questioning, I frequently ask educators to tell me about their data. What is your graduation rate? Is it measured only in 12th grade or over four years? What is the attendance rate, and how does that compare to the teacher attendance rate? In which courses are you seeing the greatest academic gains for students, and in which are you seeing the least? Which teachers or departments are succeeding with students? Do you know why? Can you demonstrate an increase in rigor in something other than the addition of Advanced Placement courses to your class offerings? If you are a "high performing" school and you peel away the data for the top 25% and the bottom 25% of your students scores, how is the "forgotten half" doing? If you have your NCLB yearly progress results, how are you doing with the subpopulations in your school? If we again imagine a room of 400 when these questions are asked, far fewer than 10 hands go up when I ask the data questions.

Do you know yours? I rest my case on data. Here is another skunk.

- Seven out of 10 high school students *nationally* do not complete the courses they need to succeed in college.
- Nearly half of our *nation's* African American population, 40% of our Latino population, and 11% of our white population attend high schools in which graduation is not the norm.

- One in 20 high school students *nationally* do not finish high school.
- Forty percent of those entering college *nationally* need remediation.
- Twenty-six percent of high school graduates *nationally* who enter four-year schools, and 45% of those who enter two-year schools, do not return to school after their first year.
- Nearly 80% of the nation's high schools identified by a recent Johns Hopkins study as having "weak promoting power" can be found in just 15 states (Arizona, California, Georgia, Florida, Illinois, Louisiana, Michigan, Mississippi, New Mexico, New York, North Carolina, Ohio, Pennsylvania, South Carolina, and Texas).
- Five southern states (Florida, Georgia, North Carolina, South Carolina, and Texas) lead the nation in the total number of schools that serve as the nation's "drop out factories." (Balfanz & Legters, 2004)

The data compel us to go beyond what Hans Meeder, former Deputy Assistant Secretary in the U.S. Department of Education under George W. Bush, calls "random acts of improvement." The stakes are too high. The data speak clearly. Our hearts should tell us, even if the data are not readily at hand, that we are failing too many of our students. While the effort to reform high schools cannot and should not be limited to urban, poor, or the most challenged of our schools, we must, as a nation, be responsible for getting education "right" for *all* students in each classroom. It is the civil rights issue of our time. We must end what former Secretary of Education Rod Paige called in March 2003 "the soft bigotry of low expectations." He insisted that educators must "let go of the myths and perceptions about who can learn and who can't" so that all children can reach high academic standards (National Right to Read Foundation, 2003).

We must ask, and answer, what I believe are the essential questions of reform work.

- Should our schools, as they are currently configured, exist?
- Do our mission statements reflect what we believe about education and what today's students need to know and be able to do?
- Do we have an absolute commitment to put into place the policies and practices that we need to meet our mission?

Is school reform only for some schools? Is it, and thus this book, only for the 15 "weak promoting power" states mentioned above, or only for high schools? I don't think so. Look at the statistics above that are designated as *national*. Some of these students are in the best of

schools. Michael Wojcik from Hackensack, New Jersey, wrote eloquently about the "quiet secret" of his high school of 1,800 students.
Hackensack High School has a 90% graduation rate and a 5% dropout
rate. However, between 25% and 35% of the students are not succeeding academically. "The failure to meet the needs of all our students is
masked by a relatively impressive list of academic accomplishments on
the part of our thriving students. Lift the mask and you see an underserved population whose members receive multiple D's and F's every
grading period."

Is being a good school good enough? It is the question, adapted from
Jim Collins's *Good to Great,* "Can a good school become a great school?"
How will we know it when we get there?

As a rule, I believe that school culture is not organized in a manner
that allows most educators to accomplish the ambitious agenda of restructuring their schools. While there should be no "cookie cutter" approach to
reform, there are, however, tried and true lessons about success in reform.
We'll work through those as we move through this book; however, it
won't be easy. In my travels I keep a magic wand in my briefcase for the
inevitable moment when a staff gets tired, or frustrated, or angry. When
they ask, "Isn't there an easy way?" I bring out the wand but explain
it doesn't work. We must have what the Finnish CEO of Nokia, Jorma
Ollila, calls "sisu." It means having the "guts" or ability to endure for the
long term to overcome all obstacles (Maney, 2004).

We will need sisu for a number of reasons. In all this time, in working closely with schools through coaching and nurturing, and through
workshops and other technical assistance support, what I have failed to
see is a system of supports that effectively sustains schools through the
sometimes gut-wrenching work of reform. Many researchers and reformers are beginning to point out that we don't have examples of a single state
or district system that has met with systemic success where all schools are
operating effectively for all students. Only a few states around the country,
notably California, Maine, Rhode Island, and Vermont, have begun to
systematically change their policies and practices affecting high schools
and to rethink the purpose, organization, and educational ideas that dom-
inate high school today. Texas is just beginning a "Comprehensive School
Reform: Texas High School Initiative," which is to serve as the umbrella
for their reform work. Louisiana has established a high school commission. Colorado has launched a statewide commission. In July 2005, the
National Governor's Association announced that after a year-long effort to
galvanize high school reform, leaders from 45 states had agreed to stan-
dardize the calculation of high school graduation rates, aiming to facilitate

comparisons and identify best practices. Baltimore, New York, and Chicago are all making strong attempts at reform. The Denver Commission on Secondary School Reform has released its findings and recommendations to improve that city's schools in their report "Not a Moment to Lose." Currently, however, a comprehensive approach that not only looks at policies and practices affecting high schools but couples that with the resources, training, accountability factors, and the mettle to see it through is lacking. It is lacking nationally and at the district and school levels. Perhaps most important, it is rare to see a system that truly dares to ask the critically important question, "What is the right educational design for today's youth?" Put most dramatically, should our schools, as currently structured, exist?

From my vantage point, I do not want to spend one more moment in a cycle that fuels educators and the communities they serve to be angry or tired or frustrated. I want schools to build their capacity, demonstrate high expectations for their students, and to operate in a culture of competence. I want to work hard, I want to succeed with schools, and I want to celebrate their success.

So, let me share what I found out about low and high expectations. A "Google" search using the phrase "low expectations" provides nearly three million hits in .29 seconds. ("High expectations" garners an additional million hits in about the same amount of time.) Interestingly enough, one of the most quoted statements about expectations comes from George W. Bush; he avows that he "is the master of low expectations—if you set a low standard you are rarely disappointed by the outcome" (Le Segretain, 2003).

Indeed, the media reflects this approach. There are low expectations for summit meetings, for space studies, for crop yields in Ohio, for United Nations negotiations, and for corporate first-quarter earnings, among other areas. Within our own industry, education, we have already documented that large numbers of students are ill-prepared to leave middle school, succeed in 9th grade, transition successfully to work, or enter college without need for remediation. And, sadly, as I have demonstrated by my data questions, most of us don't know how bad or how good our own schools are.

It is not easy to hear that we must change, that we don't have one more minute to return to "school as usual." In *Network*, Paddy Chayefsky creates Howard's famous tirade about going to the window and shouting about anger and a commitment not to take it anymore. He also has Howard saying, "I'm not going to leave you alone." That's a powerful part of the tirade. We can't leave each other alone. There is more power in our schools, in all of us combined, than in any reform model, technical assistance provider, consultant, principal, superintendent, funding stream, or mandate. We must begin to truly imagine what we want our graduates to look like and then create the schools that will create them.

I first learned this in what I thought was the most unlikely of places, rural Kansas. Over the past several years, I have had the wonderful privilege of being invited to work at Junction City High School, in Junction City, Kansas. Just to orient you if you are not familiar with Kansas, let me insert a bit of curriculum integration in the midst of a book on educational organizational change. The official Junction City Web site announces, "We're two hours from Kansas City, Wichita, and Lincoln, Nebraska, one hour from Topeka, and less than one hour from Abilene, Council Grove, Manhattan, and Salina." To this native New Yorker (the "real" Manhattan), this translates roughly into "I'm not on the east coast anymore." On my first visit, I landed at the one-gate Manhattan airport and drove the half hour to Junction with Principal Greg Springston. He affably tolerated my naïve questioning about this cattle-rich part of the world. He shared that Junction City is the home of the nation's largest U.S. Army base, Fort Riley. It was a home of the Buffalo Soldiers. It served as a true outpost for settlers as the non-native Americans moved west. It is the place where General Custer spent his last night. Greg explained that there were those in the community who joke that the town motto is "He was all right when he left here." (There, we've just covered technology, geography, transportation, careers, and social studies in a few short sentences. Now, back to reform.)

The "east coaster" in me wryly smiled that night as we sat in one of the town's few small restaurants with the school leadership team, led by teacher Mike Gross. I made the general observations that everything else in town was pretty much closed at 6:00 on a Sunday evening. I knew that I had never heard any other district refer to their school reform as needing to be as "solid as a three-legged milk stool." I wondered what real challenges they could face in this gentle corner of America. I stopped musing and started taking notes when I realized I had made some horrible prejudgments about the state of reform at this school. I knew I would learn as much from these reformers as I would bring to the process.

Greg was explaining his plan for school reform as solidly based on a commitment to *rigor, relevance, and relationships.* If any one element were not attended to, the reform would fail. The "milk stool" would tip. If anything detracted from those three elements of school improvement, they needed to be examined, fixed, or stopped. He explained that they were, as a leadership team and as a school, in the process of reinventing themselves. He laid out the intense study process of looking at their data, the national research, and the recognized reform models. In this community, in this school of more than 1,400 students, with an extraordinarily high mobility rate due to their service to Fort Riley, they were wrestling with the toughest issues about improving education. They had a diverse student population, uneven outcomes for their students, and even, sadly, a shooting on the school grounds. Principal Springston, aided by an incredibly dedicated and skilled leadership team, was leading the faculty through a series of three hard questions.

- What do we want a graduate of our school to "look" like?
- Are we producing that now?
- If we are not, what do we need to do to create that student?

Over the past six years or so, Junction City High School has answered those questions and in so doing has transformed itself. Through study and research of major reform models, they created a detailed plan that encourages engagement of all stakeholders, they created a freshman academy and upper-level career academies, and they have met with success. Principal Springston was nominated Principal of the Year for Kansas. Mike Gross was named Outstanding Career and Technical Educator 2005 for Kansas. Both would admit that it was the work of the teachers that made their successes possible. They would also admit that it's not perfect, that the work isn't done yet, that there are more things they have to work at to get the school right.

We see this same type of "Junction" questioning suggested by Rick DuFour in his work *Getting Started: Reculturing Schools to Become Professional Learning Communities*. Part of his approach centers on three general questions: "What do we want students to learn? How will we know if they learned it? What are we going to do if they do not learn it?" (Eaker, DuFour, & DuFour, 2002, p. 41) These questions direct us to a deeper question about why our particular school exists. They also lay the onus squarely on teachers to be accountable for student learning.

Asking the right questions won't be enough, nor will having the "right" answers written down. Waltrip High School in Houston, Texas, is an example of a school that is working at the deeper issues around imbedding the changes they've made into the culture of their school. They've asked the right questions and they've answered them. They have made some powerful changes in their design, in their job descriptions, and in their school structures. Now they are asking the question "How do we make the work real? How do we begin to truly embrace the culture that we have set about creating?" They have begun a broad reform effort and their question reflects an important element of building capacity—they are what I term *restless for improvement*.

It's the process of continuous inquiry, reflection, and work that begins to change the culture. When the culture changes we begin to see what Will Daggett of the International Center for Leadership in Education discovered in the spring of 2004. He was able to identify certain characteristics of schools that were "middle performing" and those that were meeting with real success. The characteristics, he said, were discernable and palpable. Here's what he discovered about schools that were meeting with success:

- There was clear evidence of small, autonomous learning communities.
- There was evidence of high expectations for all students.
- The 9th grade looked decidedly different from a traditional 9th grade.
- The 12th grade looked decidedly different from a traditional 12th grade.
- They used data at every step to guide their work.
- They utilized an effective curriculum.
- The culture supported relationships for reflective thought.
- There was an effective professional development strategy in place.
- There were leaders. (Daggett, 2004)

So, how do we get there? Research points to school reform being the most difficult type of organizational change, even more difficult if you are working at the high school level. By teacher report, those seriously committed to reform indicate that in the first two years of the process they have never worked harder, stretched themselves more, or experienced more stress. The research also points, however, to a turning point at the end of two years at which teachers experience a shared sense of success; are working smarter, not harder; and begin to see real academic gains for their students.

As educators, we take in stride the changes suggested by reform and stay optimistic. However, because of this we are sometimes guilty of a practice that Winston Churchill noted in his own work: "We go from failure to failure with enthusiasm!" Given the level of fatigue and frustration I see in so many educational systems, I believe we are at a national tipping point for educational reform. We are ready to develop the habits that will lead, finally, to success. Given the excellent work of Stephen Covey, we are used to thinking of highly effective organizations (and people, leaders, teams, families, teens, etc.) as adopting habits in groups of seven. I posit that high schools must do the same, and I suggest the following seven habits should be demonstrated by schools that want to be considered highly effective.

Highly effective schools must

1. *Demonstrate high expectations and a vision that matches them.*
Effective systems and schools are focused on the academic and personal development of students. These must be founded on a belief at the classroom, school, district, and community levels that all children can achieve at high levels. They commit to a focus that ensures not only that a child gets a strong foundation in reading, writing, math, problem solving, and critical thinking skills but that every child is respected, has an opportunity for close relationships with adults, and has an opportunity to develop his or her "voice." They recognize that learning environments must provide an atmosphere in which students are known well, are respected by caring adults, and are supported in their social and personal development. Effective schools create meaningful mission and vision statements that call every staff member to a standard of performance excellence. That mission becomes the lifeblood of their school plans and operation.

2. *Build capacity and create a true climate for success.*
Effective systems and schools are focused on a set of high expectations for their faculties and school personnel. They set a clear expectation for interactions with colleagues, students, and the community. They set a standard for the collaboration of staff in professional learning communities that look at data, shared practices, and student work. They build in, from the beginning, the capacity among teachers and administrators to "risk success," deliver high quality instruction, lead and manage classrooms and schools, use data to document continuous improvement, and provide personal support to students in ways that can help them develop foundation skills and achieve at high levels. They set an agenda and then work to empower their school leaders and teachers to meet it. Effective schools and systems reflect on the developmental needs of the individual staff members and the staff as a whole and provide opportunities for both individual and group growth. They create a staff development approach that makes sense in light of their district and school needs and the specific mission of the organization.

3. *Think small and dream big.*
Effective schools are constantly seeking new opportunities for students and staff to more effectively meet their mission. They believe that change and improvement is possible and they commit to a process of study, reflection, and work. They ask the essential question, "What is the best structure and instructional approach to meet the needs of our students?"

They create small schools, schools within schools, and personalized educational opportunities for students.

4. *Engage in legitimate community support.*

Effective schools have widespread community support from business and community leaders, postsecondary educational institutions, social service agencies, private organizations, and families. They have worked effectively at establishing a truly shared vision, partnership, and sense of shared accountability for the success of the school. They have managed to involve their stakeholders in the life of the school, giving them vitally important first-hand experience with students and teachers that makes the difference in both partner effectiveness and understanding school issues. Effective schools have developed habits that tie their partners to teachers and students in ways that build sustainability over time.

5. *Thrive with strong, sustained, and shared leadership.*

Effective schools recruit and develop strong, sustained, stable leadership at all levels—district, school, classroom, and community. They understand that leadership is not defined by job description but by an active commitment to working toward continuous improvement and engaging the entire community in that process. They share data in meaningful and straightforward ways in order that each teacher, student, family, and administrator can add to the vision, be engaged, and help implement reforms. They are honest. They ask the hard and essential questions. They are not complacent. They are in and out of each other's classrooms and offices sharing work and best practices and offering suggestions for improvement. They do not leave each other alone. The center of good leadership becomes accountability for seeing that the mission statement is alive and tangible in every aspect of the school. School leaders understand and enact the habits of highly effective schools. They plan, from the beginning, to cultivate a leadership core.

6. *Effectively align and manage resources.*

Effective schools minimize the disconnects. They have aligned their multiple plans and reports to be reflected in just one plan that is directly linked to meeting their mission. Every person in that organization knows and can articulate the plan. Effective schools have in place a practice that assesses, crosswalks, and aligns resources (and those who control them) to the mission of reform. They have learned to manage existing resources. Their budgeting and staffing reflects a commitment to their essential priorities. They have learned to use grant dollars in ways that free up monies from their general operating accounts. They have learned not to chase grant dollars but to seek resources that support their mission. In working with consultants, effective schools align each consultant's work, hold them accountable for outcomes, and make sure that their efforts are directly linked to the essential mission of the school. Effective schools have realized that their faculty is often their greatest resource. Effective schools involve their faculty and union representatives early on in reform and keep them engaged in meaningful ways in the delivery of instruction and the management of the organization.

7. *Understand time.*

Effective schools have created a sense of urgency for reform and have set a rigorous timeline that embeds the reforms in a culture of capacity and in a climate for success. Effective schools understand that the pace of simply running a high school is demanding, that the pace will not slow down, and that they cannot wait for a "good time" to start their reform. These schools have in place practices that require a regular series of checks and balances to assess each teacher's, each student's, and the overall reform's progress. They have a sense of urgency, but they have made sure that the reforms were not just superficial efforts to "get the test scores up." The focus on standards and expectations is essential. Effective schools spend time in a process of study and discovery, they create a meaningful, time-sensitive plan, and they stay the course. They do not allow the cycles of reform to deter them from their mission. Effective schools understand that there is no silver bullet, no magic wand. Becoming a great school does not happen overnight. Staying great requires constant attention.

My 5th grade teacher, Mrs. Zeigler, drilled it into us: "Good, better, best. Never let it rest. Until your good is better and your better is best!" It is time to change the course of our school reform process. We may have met with failure in the past, but we now have the ability to battle the whirring of the hamster wheel. The question now is, is this the day that you will claim as your "tipping point" or "transition point" for your classroom, school, and district? Is this the day that you will stand up and take personal responsibility? Is this the day you say, "I won't take it any more"? Is this the moment when you battle the status quo and move to becoming great?

From this day forward, we battle!

> *My great concern is not whether you have failed, but whether you are content with your failure.*
>
> —Abraham Lincoln

The Skunk Is on the Table

- Admit when you are on, perpetuating, or allowing the hamster wheel phenomenon. Break the addiction of operating in this manner. Battle!
- Follow Tony Wagner's advice: no blame, no shame, no excuses.
- Minimize "the disconnects."
- Educators must
  o Participate in a meaningful process of creating and developing professional communities in which they look at their data and use them effectively,
  o Develop plans for their schools that are attainable,
  o Refine their skills,
  o Succeed with students,
  o Study together,
  o Redefine their profession, and
  o Receive the recognition they deserve for doing well the hardest job in America.
- Take the time to develop and adhere to a coherent approach to school improvement that involves not only educational organizations but also the political, business, and community organizations that share the responsibility for developing an educated citizenry.
- Know your data.
- Know your mission statement.
- Be mad. Do not leave each other alone.
- Create schools that
  o Have clear evidence of small, autonomous learning communities,
  o Demonstrate high expectations for all students,
  o Have 9th and 12th grades that look decidedly different from traditional 9th and 12th grades,
  o Use data at every step to guide their work,
  o Utilize an effective curriculum,
  o Reflect a culture that supports relationships for reflective thought,
  o Enact an effective professional development strategy, and
  o Have true leaders.
- Strive to adopt the seven habits of highly effective schools:
  1. Demonstrate high expectations and a vision that matches them.
  2. Build capacity and create a true climate for success.
  3. Think small and dream big.
  4. Engage in legitimate community support.
  5. Thrive with strong, sustained, and shared leadership.
  6. Effectively align and manage resources.
  7. Understand time.
- Good, better, best, never let it rest, until your good is better and your better is best.

CHAPTER THREE

D.U.C.K.S. Come in F.L.O.C.K.S

If my magic wand did work, and if state departments of education, district offices, and principals had but one wish, I'd put money on that wish being that teachers would willingly engage in or "buy into" changes in instructional practices and interactions with students.

Teachers, I imagine, would use their one wish to ask that state departments of education, district offices, and principals employ strategies that allow them to actually meet the expectations set for them and then to meet with the success they envision for children. It's at least in part this disconnect in vision and responsibility that keeps us *whirring*.

In the previous chapter, we threw the skunk on the table. Sorry, the skunk stays. In this chapter, we address issues surrounding the administrators, teachers, students, communities, and consultants who are entrusted with, are living in, benefit from, are victim of, and are the future of the educational landscape. It's a chapter that focuses on hard discussions. Expect it to be messy. As Margaret Wheatley says, "change always starts with confusion" (Wheatley, 2002, p. 37). This is a chapter about understanding issues of school culture and change with a focus on authentic engagement and real "buy in." We'll begin to answer the questions about what we should do first and how we change our actions.

Organizational change theorists repeatedly tackle the issue of engagement. Indeed, "How do we get all staff to buy into reform?" is probably the question most asked of me. We know from research that in any organization a certain percentage of staff get "it" right away. Give them an idea and they'll run with it. Another percentage will just want to be told what to do, piece by piece. They'll follow along as long as it makes sense. The third group will need your special attention. Bob Slavin, of Success for All, describes the first group as "seed faculty"—plant an idea and it will flourish; the second group as "bricks"—tell them what to do and it will get done; and the third group as "sand"—you can mold it, but it won't withstand the test of time (Slavin, 1997). Add in those who will resist any change and you have the regular complement of most school faculties. For now, we should concentrate on the fact that the way you move to capacity is to have everyone involved and every voice heard.

Perhaps the second most frequently asked question I hear is "Where do we start? What do we do first?" Here, *Breaking Ranks II* offers a helpful approach.

Changing structures can be the first step in changing instruction and culture (although not the ultimate step). Others argue that the culture of the school has to change before anything else can be accomplished. Without minimizing the importance of the debate, for the purposes of [this handbook], suffice it to say that the three are highly interconnected, change is needed in all three areas, culture change must occur before change becomes truly effective. (NASSP, 2004, p. 5)

In this chapter, we'll bring this down to the school level for two reasons. First, because I believe the readers of this book, while well aware that there are political, social, and economic factors that impact our work at the district and school level, are also aware that many of these factors are beyond our specific sphere of influence as it relates to the day-to-day work we are trying to accomplish for students and schools. Second, because if Tony Wagner is right, it will take a decade to enact policy that will have a true impact on schools (Wagner, 2003, p. 129). We have to act at the school level because quite simply we can't wait through another generation of children to get school "right." Here, then, we'll focus on developing four of the habits of highly effective schools: high expectations and vision that matches them, building capacity and creating a climate for success, dreaming big and thinking small, and engaging in authentic community support.

Recently, The Colorado Children's Campaign, in part with funding from the Bill and Melinda Gates Foundation, hosted a meeting that resulted in a white paper titled *High School Conversations*. The focus of that meeting was to bring top practitioners and researchers from across the country together for an honest conversation about the status of reform work. For me, the big "take away" was the privilege of meeting Chinyelu Martin, a wonderful young California educator from the Bay Area Coalition for Equitable Schools (BAYCES). While Martin was very affirming of everyone's work, books, articles, and so on, he also challenged us, as "experts," with a question. Did we believe the following statements were true?

- There will always be a cycle of funding streams that affect schools, programs, and initiatives.
- The average stay of a superintendent will continue to be two years.
- Principals will cycle through schools almost as regularly.
- Union contracts and negotiated agreements have an impact on the way some teachers view the work.
- Some teachers, regardless of agreements, will resist any change.
- There will be an increase in our schools of students with special needs and speakers of other languages.
- Poverty will continue to exist.
- Too few parents and families are engaged in their children's education.
- Crime and violence will continue to impact our students.
- Students will continue to "present" themselves to us, to use the medical sense of that word, with a varied range of talents and abilities.

When heads nodded in agreement with this challenging set of givens—especially for our urban youth—this young reformer then asked, "Why, then, do so many plans for reform not take into account the lay of the land, *the educational landscape?*" He immediately continued with a metaphor likening the process of reform to a geographical landscape. "If we are standing on the coast of California and looking toward Hawaii, we don't say, 'Hawaii has a problem, it is far away. Let's build a bridge to get there.' We understand, based on the landscape, that a bridge is impractical and we must use another approach to get where we need to be. We accept that *there is nothing wrong with Hawaii; there would be something wrong with the approach of building a bridge to get there.*"

"If this is the case," Martin continued, "why, then, do we not take fully into account the educational landscape we are faced with and understand that it demands a different and specific course of action? Why do we continue to develop systems without looking at the landscape of our schools and our children?"

Whirr, whirr, whirr.

I was dumbstruck. Were the challenges we were facing in effective reform implementation so directly tied to the fact that we were not truly taking stock of the environmental landscape in which we were trying to succeed? Since that moment, I've been looking at the landscape. In candid discussions with principals and my colleague reformers, I venture to say that many of us have been working with blinders on, or at least we haven't been taking into account the real implications of the landscape of each individual community's strengths and deficits on reform. As we saw with my Maryland school example, even when we have the gift to begin a new school we get mired down in simply re-creating what we know. We too often create what one of my colleague reformers calls redesigned "schools in drag."

Even when we get "out of the box," the history of how we have operated schools in the past haunts us. Most recently, I was discussing a new small school start-up with a colleague. Her new effort had the blessing of funders and the school system and was being created based on strict and widely accepted reform practices. During the planning months, they paid painstaking attention to the development of a school leadership team, selected specific curriculum and instructional strategies, and mounted a strong student and family orientation. When I asked how the new school was going now that they were two months into operation, she shared that the new school of just 140 students had already lost teachers based on the district's allowable teacher-per-student ratio. It was already struggling to maintain the high expectations set before they opened. When I asked her why she thought all their planning was not being met with the anticipated outcome, her response was, "Well, it is still an urban school." *Whirr . . .*

We see some of this same phenomenon being played out in the recent University of Chicago Consortium of School Research study on the impressive small schools movement in Chicago. Their report highlights that the new schools are still beleaguered by the reputations of their former large comprehensive high school selves. Students still arrive reading significantly below grade level, the same teachers are employed and get caught in a cycle of traditional habits, and the leadership is focused on the demands of opening and operating a new school rather than on instructional practices (Dell'Angela, 2004).

There have now been enough school reconstitutions to prove that it isn't enough simply to close one structure and expect the new one to open and meet high expectations. Although the research bears out that it is far easier to create a personalized, professional teaching and learning community with high academic expectations for students in new schools than in those that are being redesigned into small learning communities, it isn't that simple, and it certainly is not a promise of improvement. Don't, however, be deterred. None of this is an indictment, or even a foreshadowing, of failure because there is also excellent news in the Chicago study and in individual examples across the country. As Margaret J. Wheatley points out in *Turning to One Another: Simple Conversations to Restore Hope to the Future*, "The cure for despair is not hope. It's discovering what we want to do about something we care about" (Wheatley, 2002, p. 19). The Chicago schools are already seeing evidence of increased attendance, fewer instances of violence, closer relations between students and staff members, and more help available to students. And the staffs believe that more students are now aspiring to college enrollment (Dell'Angela, 2004).

Chinyelu Martin's words about the landscape urge a design that is capable of delivering the high expectations we set for students and that responds to the needs of the students and the community at the deepest level. Our restructuring efforts must establish and utilize a plan for getting there that does the same. The plan must be one that deals head on with the real challenges of the reform work: the challenge of changing an educational culture that is pathetically slow to change.

Changing culture and believing our expectations can become realities takes time. Indeed, Paul Kelleher and Marya R. Levenson, with more than 30 years of combined experience as superintendents, looked at the issue of changing educational practice and its impact on student achievement. They threw the skunk on the table and asked, "Can school culture change?" Recognizing that the "intractability of school organizations exists," they highlighted that the pace of and attempts at importing (rather than developing internally) a school culture have sometimes developed into a school's sense that they are incompetent to handle reform. While the authors answer their culture change question with a qualified "yes," they also point out that "if culture deals with how people perform their work, then changes in culture must involve new patterns of work" (Kelleher & Levenson, 2004). A change in culture comes about by a change in practice; it comes about by developing habits of effectiveness.

Which brings us to the ducks. Several years ago, I had the great opportunity to hear Neila Connors, author of *If You Don't Feed the Teachers They Eat the Students* (2000), speak in Oklahoma. In case you are unfamiliar with the suburbs of Oklahoma City, let me, again, offer a parenthetical point of reference. I am not sure where the heart of the Bible belt is, but suburban Oklahoma City must be pretty much dead center. The night I arrived, Oklahoma City glowed off to the right in the night sky as I drove west on U.S. Route 40. Three large office buildings had their lights turned on and off in a pattern that displayed three large crosses. It's a pattern that was originally displayed after the horrific Oklahoma City bombing and was resurrected after the events of 9/11. While impressed at the citywide coordination of displayed support, I was also aware that it was the Jewish high holy day of Yom Kippur. I wondered at the lack of inclusion, and I puzzled about how hard it would be to work a Star of David into the building light matrix. The next morning at the school, I seemed to be the only one who was surprised when one of the principals, preparing to introduce Ms. Connors, opened the professional development session with a reading from the Christian New Testament Book of Corinthians. Immediately, I thought about the landscape and how in this corner of America, religion—Christian religion—was a firm part of the public school culture.

I was musing about the implications of this on school policy when I was captivated by Connors's strong message about teacher responsibility. While I sometimes get bogged down in lofty language on this issue, citing research and articles on new and veteran teachers, suggesting that we spend too much time chasing the energy of the slow to change 5%, or urging that a few recalcitrant teachers not be allowed to hold a school reform effort hostage, Connors had a much more direct approach. With her wonderful sense of humor, she suggested that, indeed, there were always going to be complainers or naysayers or detractors in any faculty. To Connors, these are "the ducks," those individuals who are Determined to Undermine, Criticize, and Kill Success. She gave wonderful examples of hearing them at meetings, "Quack, quack, I don't think this is going to work." "Quack, quack, we tried this before." "Quack, quack, I'm unhappy with. . . . (fill in the blank)."

She shared that in school meetings you often have to allow for the diffusion of the tension and the letting go of the baggage of the day, but you can't allow the negativity to take over the meeting. In her school experience, she allowed the first five minutes of any meeting to be "in the duck pond." After that, things got serious and fines were paid if you "wandered into the pond." If I remember her story correctly, she shared that one day she was in a foul (or perhaps fowl) mood, walked into a meeting, tossed $20 in the middle of the table and said she was taking up the whole meeting because she was mad at everyone.

Every organization has a few of these folks. The ducks too often distract us because so often they are the most vocal. They also, sometimes, have a lot to tell us about what works and doesn't in the schoolhouse. I do a lot of listening in schools. A number of years ago, I remember excitedly listening to the message of a new principal in Washington, D.C. She shared her enthusiasm for being at the school, recognized the value of the teachers, and said she wanted to listen to them as she was sure they knew that sweeping changes would be taking place across the District. I was sitting next to an English teacher of 20 years. She muttered that she was on her seventh principal, and that she was sure that she, the English teacher, would outlast any reform and this particular principal. I was appalled at her comments, thinking her a recalcitrant teacher. She added that she was just going back to her classroom to teach. Was her attitude about getting back to her classroom evidence of burnout or a well-honed strategy not to burn out? That encounter was 15 years ago, and that teacher retired just as this book was going to press. She had outlasted at least five additional principals and a cycle of reforms. The truth is she wasn't a duck—she knew what was coming; she understood the landscape.

The landscape can, indeed, be treacherous. In a former factory town suburb of Boston I cut my consultant eyeteeth on the challenge of the union agreement. This is a much-skirted issue in the work surrounding reform, but in the spirit of that skunk still being on the table, let me share the hazards of not taking the time up front to engage all stakeholders. It was October and the New England fall colors blazed brightly. My team entered the school, had a great meeting with the principal and project coordinator, and were well prepared for our start-up meeting with the faculty. We were told that more than 70% of the faculty had voted for a reform that would require they move from their classrooms into new areas of the building, utilize a specific curriculum, and begin to work in teams. To my team's mind, this redesign would require intense planning time and a huge culture shift. Our suggestion was that after this initial kick-off meeting we would begin in earnest in a few weeks with a second 90-minute afterschool meeting. We never got there. The issue of time and the union contract derailed us.

In this school, the teacher contract provided for teachers to stay 10 minutes past the final student bell four days per week for the purpose of closing out the day, meeting with students, preparing for the next day, and so on. On Fridays, faculty could leave with the students. During that initial full-faculty meeting, we spent almost the full 90 minutes trying to figure out how to work the reform process into the contracted time. We discussed options for "buying back" the time by allowing the teachers to leave with the students every day for eight days, which would provide the time for the suggested next meeting. We got tripped up, thinking that the 10 minutes from the ninth day would "count" and we could hold a 90-minute meeting. What we were told was that the faculty would have to actually be released for nine days with the students, or we would be taking 10 minutes of their contracted time. At the end of this start-up, 90-minute filibuster meeting, and exactly at the scheduled time for the close of the meeting, the faculty voted with their feet and left for the day. Reform work at the school was effectively stalled. Shortly afterwards, the principal and superintendent were replaced. *Whirr. Whirr. Whirr.*

I cannot help but think that we certainly needed a better sense of the landscape before walking into that system and that the principal needed a far better understanding of what a vote meant to that faculty. We could have worked much more productively for that group of teachers if we had had meaningful discussions about what the real issues were prior to that painful meeting. In my experiences from Massachusetts to Illinois, I can attest that while the "union issue" can quickly turn into an "us vs. them," that is rarely the intent. The challenges arise because there is some disconnection between communication, trust, data, goals, needs, and action. I always recommend that any work around reform immediately involve discussions and involvement of the union and building representatives. Their perspective and assistance in design can make all the difference in how the faculty as a whole feels honored and respected. Their participation can prevent the waste of what we have so little of, time.

After the union experience in Massachusetts, I committed to borrowing, with full credit, directly from Neila Connors's talk. The ducks have to be recognized. There are now groups of educators across the country that I've worked with that very quickly control the negativity or sidetracking of a meeting by simply muttering "quack, quack, quack, quack, quack." No ducks allowed. These individuals, while they may indeed be excellent teachers in their own classrooms, can keep us on the hamster wheel. Perhaps they have been the victims of what one researcher calls "the carousel of school reform," where principals, superintendents, and mandates change in a given cycle. Given "the landscape" and the way so many reform efforts have rolled out, can we really blame the ducks for their "this too shall pass" attitudes? While we can't blame them, we also can't allow their duckishness to derail our need to change practice—our commitment to continuously improve.

As we move deeper into the work on engagement, we conduct multiple focus groups, have questions raised and answered, and begin to peel back to the real issues. We build true teams and take the time to assess each other's strengths and weaknesses. We ask hard questions about our schools' or districts' collective assets. We hold messy conversations about what it means for all of us to be on board with the reform. These hard conversations, coupled with real data, open the door for deeper work. Without a data component, they reflect only the "moment in time" or snapshot of the district's or school's overall readiness for, or involvement in, reform. Yet these conversations provide critical information.

I had the opportunity to share Connors's idea about the ducks while working with educators along the 100-mile-long Louisiana Bayou LaFourche. The dedicated teachers and administrators of LaFourche Parish Schools were taking a hard look at their data; they were beginning to look at student work and teacher assignments, as The Education Trust and others so expertly coach us to do. In doing so they found themselves asking, as many systems do, "Why do our 'ducks' seem to come in 'flocks'?" Not to be outdone by Ms. Conners, they challenged themselves to flesh out a "flocks" acronym. After they wrestled with a series of tries at an appropriate "F" word, they determined that their ducks were simply *F*olks *L*acking *O*pportunities, *C*reativity, *K*nowledge, and *S*kills. With that acronym a new approach to staff engagement in the process of reform was born. We had to provide the ducks with the right opportunities, tap their creativity, and design staff development and individual professional learning opportunities that addressed knowledge and skill gaps. Their voices were important. Surrounding ourselves with just the "yes" people was more comfortable but, like Michael Fullan says, surrounding yourself with these educators is "not a bad strategy for getting through the day, but it is a lousy one for getting through the implementation dip" (Fullan, 2001, p. 42). Just like all stakeholders, the ducks have to have an authentic part in the process. If they trust they can build it, they will come.

I've already laid out that at GMS Partners our approach to high school improvement focuses on just five things: data-driven decisions, personalization, curriculum, partnership, and the creation of a climate for success. We usually begin that process at either the school or district level by looking at a five-stage process, recognizing that in schools the process is rarely a linear one. The stages for the work are formation, study and awareness, engagement and commitment, establishing structures, and evaluation. The formation and study and awareness process begins with developing a culture of high expectations and vision. It is the essential question of what we and our students should expect our schools to be. At these stages we follow a very simple and straightforward process. We borrow from Junction City High School. We begin with a group, usually appointed by the principal or the superintendent. Often it is a school improvement committee; sometimes it is a state or district committee looking at reform. The group should, at minimum, consist of teachers, principals, guidance counselors, department chairs, special educators, the master scheduler, and union representatives. Student, family, and community members are an added bonus. If you are lucky enough to have support from your local education fund (LEF), their participation should also be solicited. We begin by asking the question, "What should a graduate of our schools 'look' like?"

The committee usually notes student outcomes such as passing the state test, being ready for postsecondary experiences, being able to manipulate and use technology, being lifelong learners, being polite and respectful, and demonstrating good moral character. Almost uniformly, there is little attention to the detail of students performing at or above grade level; demonstrating their knowledge, skills, and abilities; participating in college-level classes; or using critical thinking skills. There is usually little connection to the mission statement espoused by the school or district. The exercise rarely uncovers a level of deep thought about how to address the needs of English language learners or students with special needs, or those entering school performing significantly below grade level, but it is a start. Tony Wagner notes a similar challenge in his work when asking school leaders to articulate a need for reform. He notes "how thin and inarticulate some of the responses are" when it comes to describing the need for change. He wonders if the leaders can't articulate the need for change, how then can the teacher pool embrace it? (Wagner, 2003, p. 136).

Providing common language around expectations for graduates creates a point of entry that is essential to round out a group's early thinking about reform work. It provides the launch pad that propels the group to ask the hard question, "What does our data tell us about the success we are making in 'producing' the student we have envisioned?" It is an amazing transformation in the group when they begin to discuss in what small measure they are meeting their own expectations.

From this vantage point we begin to create a framework for our first habit, high expectations and a vision that matches them. When groups begin to create their ideal student and analyze the data, they begin to own the process of creating that student. Internationally, we can look through the eyes of Marc Tucker, president of the National Center for Education and Economy, to the systems of Denmark and Singapore for schools that reflect high standards. In these countries, "high standards and expectations are understood by students across grade levels and mesh with the expectations of university and business leaders." In Singapore, "schools routinely place their best teachers with their lowest performing students." In Denmark, "typical vocation students know three languages, theoretical math, probability and statistics, and solid sciences" (Allen, 2004).

I've come to believe that while every school must determine what footprint it wishes to leave in its community, there are also operational practices that we should expect our secondary schools to follow.

- The mission statement is at the heart of the work. Schools need a clear and concise mission that can be articulated by everyone in the school community. The mission statement is the main thing and you must, in the words of David Cottrell, "keep the main thing the main thing" (Cottrell, 2002, p. 27). The main thing must be inclusive of the needs of all students and be in synch with the needs of the business and university communities.

- Faculty and staff work in an atmosphere that is inclusive and respectful of all participants and where they are empowered to enact the mission. There must be a true sense of participatory governance and shared accountability for the decisions, policies, and practices that are in place to meet the mission. The process for decisions is reflective, open, and honest.
- Faculty and staff are committed to the use of data, a process of reflection, and a continuous improvement of their instructional practice that includes a professional development plan that makes sense.
- The leadership encourages measured risks and understands that failure is an opportunity to learn more.
- The school structure supports a clear sense of autonomy, identity, personalization, instructional focus, and accountability for learners and leaders alike.

I further believe that we should be able to see a direct payoff for these practices in the quality of students' lives at school and in their academic achievement. I believe we should expect that students will benefit from this climate by being deeply engaged as members who help shape it. I believe that the culture should encourage students and their families to expect that they will receive (not hope to receive) the following:

- A rigorous curriculum that is reflected in standards and practice for all students. A curriculum that is measured not only by the number of Advanced Placement courses and dual-credit opportunities but also by rigor in every classroom where teachers teach and students are engaged in learning.
- A curriculum and learning sequence that offers true options for all students to find their passion and to conduct their learning beyond the walls of the classroom with multiple opportunities for independent learning, guided research, and multiple forms of assessment.
- A guidance and advisory system that ensures that each student is known well by adults and is encouraged to take higher-level classes, is college-ready, and is coached to understand the ramifications of high school and postsecondary choices on further study and work.
- A climate that encourages each student's voice to be heard.
- The extra help necessary to succeed and excel at high school.

Students and their families should come to expect a truly personalized learning environment. And "personalization means more than talking to and caring about some students. It means creating formal structures that ensure that all students receive personal care, attention, and support" (Silva & Mackin, 2002, p. 148).

During the study and awareness process, teachers begin to imagine this type of experience for students and momentum is gained. There is now a core group of individuals who "get it," even if there have been no structural decisions, requested changes in instructional practices, or policies changed. As Wheatley states,

> change doesn't happen from a leader announcing a plan. Change begins from deep inside a system, when a few people notice something they will no longer tolerate, or respond to a dream of what's possible. We just have to find a few others who care about the same thing. (Wheatley, 2002, p. 25)

It's a beginning; the next step is the point where the battle can be lost or won.

Here is where we must take the time to look at part of the second habit of highly effective schools, building capacity. It is time to move past the choir and get the whole congregation singing. It's about clear communication and inclusion in the conversation. With respect to the potential for bruised feelings and propensity for entrenchment that we've already noted, let's be clear that capacity building is not just about the teachers. Capacity, as we define it, is evidence of a critical mass in an institution that is agile enough to be strategic and tactical in managing its own growth and development. School improvement requires that everyone's job description be on the table. Changing culture, as we learned earlier, means a changed way of operation. Everyone from the top down, bottom up, and on the sidelines has to be involved in the process. Central administration, guidance, teachers, department chairs, union representatives, librarians, special educators, career and technical educators, AP teachers, coaches, and principals all should be reexamining their roles. The skunk on the table here is that I have never done a staff development where there was not a consensus that the school's greatest asset was "the faculty." It doesn't take long, maybe just a walk down the hallway, before someone, however, will come up and say, "You know, our best asset is the faculty, except for maybe the [fill in the blank] department." Unless, of course, you are a member of the aforenamed department; then the weakness, of course, is some other department. Currently, in my experience, it is not at all uncommon for the guidance staff or the department chairs to urge change in all operations of the school with the exception of theirs.

As you begin to wrestle with roles and responsibilities, expect messy conversations. To use Wheatley's terminology, "be willing to be disturbed" (Wheatley, 2002, p. 34). Jimmy Carter is credited with saying, "If you fear making anyone mad then you ultimately probe for the lowest common denominator of human achievement." This is where the real work begins. I have a colleague at the Council of Chief State School Officers who says he always tries to "do the hard things once." Dealing with the "ugly" conversations, as we sometimes call them, head-on avoids a lot of the "parking lot" and "faculty room" discussions that sometimes undermine reform.

Reform is not comfortable, and it's especially uncomfortable for educators who come to the profession, at least in part, because it is a known culture with set ways of operation. Indeed, in understanding the landscape, we must understand who comes to the teaching profession. Tony Wagner points out that many in education are risk averse, consider themselves "craftsmen" with a specific expertise at creating a product, and enjoy working alone. He further points out that the very structure of our schools promotes classroom autonomy and individual isolation that leads to a diminished capacity for change (Wagner, 2002, pp. 131–133). Many educators lived this pattern of existence during their own high school years and expect it to continue as we work in high schools today. But this is not *our* high school experience. It belongs to a new type of student with needs far different from the ones we had. These students need to thrive differently in high school and be prepared to excel in a world none of us can anticipate. As the efforts for reform deepen, be prepared for a great deal of discomfort, and be prepared to deal with it.

You already know that I am math averse, but the truth is that one of the first steps in engagement has to be about the research and the numbers. That said, there are probably few educators whose passion is going to be ignited by the carrot of increased standardized test scores. It is too easy in data discussions to imagine that the indicators refer to someone else's classroom or a school other than our own. A data review without making connections to specific classrooms and practices is irrelevant. It does not result in motivation to action; instead, too often it becomes information overload for staff. Educators have to see what my colleague Judy Neal calls the WIFMs—what's in it for me. A discussion of the connection between whole school, classroom, and individual students and teacher data brings to light a pattern that allows schools to see the true picture of who is failing, who is underperforming, and which departments are succeeding with which students. A telling discussion on data might unveil that students are failing geometry, as an example, because so many students are exiting algebra with a "D." This should develop into a discussion of the merit of passing a class with a D. Does it really qualify a student to do upper-level work? This can lead to a deeper discussion on strategies and recommendations for the extra help students may need. Ultimately, it can lead to a faculty understanding where there are areas of success and causes for celebration. In a like manner, as patterns of failures and the development of needed supports emerge, the data becomes a guiding force in the redesign work in every classroom. Ultimately, the changes are about empowerment and teacher ownership of the reform. It results in an increased enjoyment of teaching as students meet with greater success (the real teacher motivator). These WIFMs provide opportunities for teachers to serve as mentor teachers, to coach students to success, and to feel empowered. But faculties will need help to get there.

It is ironic that in working with schools there is one uniform first request for support—"professional development." Like Wagner's "thin and inarticulate responses," I have found that when probed on what this means, what training is needed, what specific need will be addressed, or what the expected outcome is, it is rare that educators can articulate the specifics. It is a further irony that one of the highest levels of frustration for educators is professional development.

The National Commission on Teaching and America's Future stated,

> Most professional development dollars are spent either reimbursing teachers for courses that may or may not be directly related to school needs or their classroom responsibilities, or for district-determined workshops with even less connection to the teachers' own practice. As traditionally organized, in-service education—usually conducted as mass-produced hit and run workshops—is not well suited to helping teachers with the most pressing challenges they face in deepening their subject matter knowledge, responding to student diversity, or to teaching more effectively. (National Commission on Teaching and America's Future, 1996)

Schools that commit to setting a high standard for professional practice, using many of DuFour's professional learning community strategies or Critical Friends Group protocols, begin to design their own professional development based on their own and their collective knowledge gaps as they relate to "the main thing"—the organization's mission. They also design the time for the practices to be followed up, the time for the desired change in practice to be worked on and for it to become a habit.

I believe all teachers should develop their own Individual Education Plan, not for the purpose of evaluation but for the purposes of continuous improvement. I don't think, for example, it makes me less of a skilled consultant if I admit there are still things I am learning about scheduling or that my personal Individual Education Plan has placed a basic mastery of Spanish at the top of the list.

If it's any comfort, there are few who really know what it means to work in a school that consistently strives to achieve the vision we've described above. In the everyday running of schools it is simply too easy to slip back into old practices. But there are schools that are working successfully toward this thing we call capacity. We see it demonstrated

- When a staff collectively is able to demonstrate that they have the knowledge and comprehension of the strategies needed for reform,
- When they see their place in it, and
- When they see that they can and will transform that information into a changed structure, changed instruction, and changed operational practice.

Capacity begins at the moment when, as Brenda Craige, project director for the federal Small Learning Community grant at Will Rogers High School in Tulsa, Oklahoma, says, "we understand the meaning between good practice and where we want to go with our students." It begins with understanding and results in a willingness to engage in the process. It's about stepping off the wheel as a critical mass of educators and creating habits of effectiveness.

There is, of course, the question of whether we have a critical mass and whether we have the right faculty for the redesign work at hand. Can they rise to the challenge or do they need to be encouraged to find a transfer placement? In Jim Collins's *Good to Great* world, this is the hard question not of having staff, but of having the right staff in the right jobs (Collins, 2001, p. 61). Moving staff out of the schoolhouse, sadly, needs to be a real consideration. Michael Fullan urges "counseling out or otherwise ridding the school of teachers who persistently neglect their own learning" (Fullan, 2003, p. 77). In multi-school districts, or in ones without a coordinated reform strategy, it is far easier to encourage a teacher to switch to a school that may be more in keeping with his or her educational practice. In a one– or two–high school town these discussions are much more difficult. We rely on the critical mass and a coordinated system, both at the school and district levels, to encourage all educators to support the reform. Our task is getting them passionate about redefining themselves and best serving students. The simple truth, however, is that some educators will not support the desired improvements, and they need to be encouraged to find a setting that suits their talents and philosophy.

But what does all this quacking and posturing tell us? That there are loyalties within school structures that can be capitalized on and built upon, that there is a commitment to the profession, and that people are passionate about their work. "There is no power for change greater than the community discovering what it cares about" (Wheatley, 2002, p. 48). We must stay the course and stand firm on where we, collectively, believe our school can go based on the expectations we have set.

When we really get this part right, this is the point at which educators have the voice to say, "We set a standard for how we are going to operate [our high expectations]; we have the knowledge, skills, and ability to get it right; we are accountable [we have capacity]; now let us dream and build our school." The process of study and awareness has nurtured a sense of empowerment. Success begins to reap a sense of trust in the process. The work begins to become its own intrinsic reward, and educators are ready to dream big and think small.

While, again, no linear pattern of growth can be assumed, the next stage of work is about establishing the curricular and structural elements that are the true heart of reform and school improvement. If reviewing and refining the mission statement has really become the main thing, and teachers have owned the process of creating their ideal graduate, the next steps, while rife with details, are easy in comparison. The right mission, one that is truly embraced as real, will serve as the best compass for this work. You know the direction; the question becomes what do we need to get "there." Now it is no longer about creating boutique programs for some students. It is about creating a school environment that challenges the existence of specialty programs for the gifted or chosen few and asks how we make that type of experience available to the many. It is not about limiting opportunities but about opening up your thinking. I used to refer to this, as many do, as "thinking outside the box" until I had the opportunity to discuss school improvement with Charles Sturdivant, deputy superintendent for Grand Rapids Michigan Public Schools. He provided a more useful approach. He stated that in looking at strategies and structure to meet the high expectations and needs of today's students, he didn't want his educators to think outside the box; he wanted them to see "there is no box." We must create schools that never existed before.

Dreaming big entails creating the high school you always imagined for yourself and for your students. What does instruction look like? What types of experiences in and out of the classroom should students have? How do you really personalize the environment for student academic and personal support and for student voices really to be heard? How are families and communities involved in the design of the educational experience? How do you really adequately prepare students for a future that has them succeed at work, ongoing education, and life? What are the expectations for faculty and administrators? How will you use time (schedules) to accomplish all you want? What types of exhibitions, portfolios, and senior projects make for positive culminating experiences? What is the right management structure? How do all members of the school community serve as leaders?

Answering these big questions by not only putting job descriptions but also routine practices on the table almost always brings us to "small." The research is unquestionable; true change and true improvement in the culture and quality of teaching and learning happens when large schools redefine themselves as small. There are ample resources on why and how to do this work. In the next chapter, we will look at aspects of leadership and plan development that will support the school's transformation. Here, suffice it to say that unequivocally the large comprehensive high school cannot well serve the needs of all students. By becoming small, either in terms of school size or in terms of creating smaller learning communities, we have a real chance at bringing good teaching to the fore and developing a true shared leadership structure in the educational setting. Small schools and small learning communities are places where students can't hide and neither can underperforming teachers and administrators.

"Getting small" has its own set of tough questions if we are not going to simply re-create what we once knew as the American high school. The schools with the biggest challenges, the dropout factories, have to make the most difficult choices, for example, whether to keep sports. Let me be clear that I don't believe that sports programs and high academics are mutually exclusive and there has to be an either/or choice. However, if our main thing is academic success, we have to have the difficult discussions and we have to balance the health and motivating factors of sports with a mission that states that students succeed academically. There are now schools sacrificing a sports team (and band and other elective courses) to put resources into programs that ensure student academic success. The issue of size, then, is more than structural; it is about the resources used to ensure academic and personal success for students. If everything is really on the table, from the length of the school day to who teaches which classes and whether there should be a school football team, we realize, as Sturdivant does, that *there is no box.*

And, finally, we get to students. In developing schools that are committed to the fourth habit of highly effective schools, engaging in authentic community support, we address not only student voices but also the voices of families, community partners, and consultants.

Often, when I urge the inclusion of students in the reform process, I am met with hesitancy. When I urge that we must have a representative sample of students—the truant, the repeater, the "ideal graduate," the special education student, and the English language learner—I am frequently met with the concern that it will take too long to bring them up to speed and engage them effectively in the process. When I ask for a focus group and tell the administration I am going to ask the students to create their "ideal teacher," I see raised eyebrows. They know that one of my questions to the students will be "How many of your teachers meet that description?" Listening to students has always been an essential element of my work. Conducting student focus groups has always helped me put my finger on the real pulse of the school. There you find out all sorts of things about policy and practices. Kids are honest, even if their experience sometimes limits their full understanding of the reasons for certain policies. They almost always hold the answer to some questions that the adults are wrestling with. Let me share some examples.

- In Salina, Kansas, the district had mandated Silent Sustained Reading (SSR), and the student council and school administration each had materials they needed to get into the hands and under the noses of students. It was the students who made the obvious suggestion to have the materials presented during SSR.
- Also in Salina, students complained that since the school had been renovated, there was no longer a locker next to the office that was designated as a student suggestion box. It hadn't been a deliberate attempt at limiting student voice; the locker designation had simply been left off the renovation checklist. The suggestion locker was up and operational in a few days because of the students' observation.
- In a suburb of Chicago, I asked young men why their peers were dropping out of school in record numbers. They said it was because there was no reason for them to stay; no one really wanted them in school anyway. Supports for young men were developed and faculty awareness increased.
- In Washington, D.C., students had the opportunity to work half a day and go to school half a day. As the adults, we made what seemed the natural assumption that students should come to school first and then go to their jobs. We didn't take into account afterschool activities,

two sets of bus and train commutes, and employer dissatisfaction with students arriving late or needing to leave early to get back to school. When conflict arose, we led with punishing the students for not getting back and forth in time. It was a student who suggested that if the students went to their jobs first thing in the morning, they could save money and commuting time. They also pointed out they would be more focused on each aspect of their day because they wouldn't be worrying about the commute. Based on this insight, we were able to make a scheduling switch in the second semester that increased student performance and employer satisfaction. (The problem wasn't with Hawaii; it was in how we were approaching getting there!)

It is amazing to me that so many educators, either in formal advisory programs or in more informal settings, are still so hesitant to interact with students outside of the formal classroom setting. While learning to listen to students' voices, I suggest that schools listen to the words of Phyllis Hunter, president of Phyllis C. Hunter Consulting, Inc. I heard Mrs. Hunter speak several years ago in Washington, D.C. During her talk she asked us to raise our hands if we were parents. She asked us to keep our hands raised if we sent our children to school. She told us to keep our hands raised if we only sent our best children to school. Amid our quizzical stares and raised hands, she pushed on. She asked if we sent only our best children to school, what we did we do with the other ones, leave them at home? No, she pointed out, like parents everywhere we send the best kids we have to school and they need to be welcomed into our schoolhouse as just that. Each child, each best child a family has at home, deserves to be educated and to be heard.

I do ask students to "build their ideal teacher." As with other aspects of their schools, they are remarkably insightful. They want teachers who are fair and honest, who are hard on them, and who set clear expectations. They want teachers who know their subject matter and use multiple forms of assessment. They want teachers to understand that some of them like to draw, or do research, or talk, or demonstrate their skills in a variety of ways. They want to do more group work and projects. They want to apply what they are taught. They want a pacing system that makes sense. They want time for extra help. They want a teacher who cares about them. They want to be respected. They want school rules to make sense and to be applied consistently. More and more I hear they want teachers who are happy and like their job. When I ask how many of their teachers meet this ideal—many, few, or none—the range is almost always in the few to none category.

It's a skunk on the table, and it opens all sorts of cyclical hamster wheel–like discussions. When I share this information with the school faculty, too often teachers identify their own practice with the ideal teacher, identify others as not hitting the mark, and do not engage in introspection that can lead to their own professional growth. Too often I have heard "I'll respect kids when they start respecting me." *Whirr, whirr, whirr.*

The fact is that too many of our students don't have the experience of great teaching. These are our best kids; they deserve our best schools. This window into the student experience should serve as a motivator to educators to reflect on practice.

In a like manner to school size, much has been written about family involvement and community partnerships. Inclusion of families (no matter how they are defined), community and faith-based organizations, and businesses and postsecondary institutions are critical if the reform is going to be inclusive of all stakeholders. The work in this area must be about creating true partnerships, not merely about establishing relationships. These voices, too, need to be heard and validated as they bring to the reform not only coveted resources but a perspective and knowledge base that cannot be seen from the vantage point of the schoolhouse.

In addition to the community members mentioned above, there is an often-overlooked participant in the partnership process—the consultant, or the multiple consultants who help schools and districts in the reform process. As a consultant, I have always worked to establish my role as a true partner in the reform—not surprising, perhaps, given the name of the company, GMS Partners. Prior to working with a school, we ask for minutes of meetings, Web page links, and access to data; we try to get to know the school in its entirety. When serving schools locally, we volunteer for their business advisory boards and we go to graduations. We attempt, as often as possible, to make the type of investment in the school or district that they are making in us. In our opinion, it's what good consulting looks like. Too often schools engage in "drive by" or disconnected consultant support. They don't look at establishing a long-term consultant relationship with set benchmarks for performance. In schools with multiple consultants, there is rarely an attempt at aligning the work of one with the other—or even a practice of informing consultants about who else is working in the building and for what purpose. The consultant can serve many purposes, from a second set of eyes on a given challenge; to technical support in a specific area of need such as literacy, team building, or evaluation; to someone who will roll up her sleeves and partner on creating materials, plans, and reports; to motivator and workshop provider; to long-term coach. Most of the time our job is to help hold your feet to the fire that you have set and provide the support to help you succeed. Consultants engage in all of these efforts but should never do so without asking how their work relates to the mission of the organization, what specific goal the school is trying to accomplish, who else is working in the school or district—and whether they can spend some time talking with others about their efforts. We do all of this and also ask how we can be involved in the long haul. For us, the unrelated "drive by" approach is almost always a source of confusion, mixed messages, and a source of disconnects for educators. Educators quickly see it as one more thing that will not be followed up. It's a perfect excuse to keep *whirring*.

This secondary school transformation work is not for the faint of heart. I absolutely believe that teachers and administrators can create schools in which there is a focus on excellence. We may not be able to change the landscape, but we can change our schools and how we operate as a teaching and learning community. If we don't believe this we shouldn't be in the business. This puzzle called school reform doesn't fit unless we bring all teachers together and ask them to lead the mission. We must have at the very core of this work a leadership team in the school that understands the mission is to serve all students to high standards, works hard, and communicates with and engages all stakeholders. This requires a variation on Jim Collins's *Good to Great* question. Why do we exist? Do we have the design of our schools right? Effective reform cannot happen by tinkering around the edges; it demands a systemic change in practice.

If we are going to see real reform we must all serve as leaders in our schools—and while I am a firm believer that principal leadership makes a critical difference in the school, the schools with the greatest success have a climate of a professional learning community in which all teachers take ownership of the results, share each other's work, and commit to a process of continued growth. We tackle this issue in the next chapter.

> *Make no friendship with an elephant-keeper if you have no room to entertain an elephant.*
>
> —Saadi of Shiraz as quoted in *Entertaining an Elephant*, William McBride (1997)

D.U.C.K.S. Come in F.L.O.C.K.S

- Involve everyone in the reform dialogue. Let every voice be heard.
- Focus on structure and instruction simultaneously; know that if you don't change the culture—the beliefs, policies, and practices—the changes to instruction and structures won't take hold.
- Act at the school level because, quite simply, you can't wait through another generation of children to get school "right."
- Build plans that reflect, can be implemented in, and can achieve results in your educational landscape.
- Discover what you want to do about something you care about.
- Recognize that a change in culture requires a change in practice.
- Recognize, listen to, and learn from *the ducks;* however, don't let them take the reform process hostage.
- Develop meaningful opportunities for *the flocks,* those who lack opportunities, creativity, commitment, or sufficient knowledge and skills.
- Create a process for reform that includes building a leadership core committed to study and awareness, engagement and commitment, establishing structures, and evaluation.
- Ask the hard questions about what a graduate should look like, whether you are producing that now, and what you need to do to get there.
- Guarantee students and their families schools where there is
  - A rigorous curriculum that also offers true options for all,
  - A guidance and advisory system that ensures that each student is known well by adults and is encouraged to take higher-level classes, is college-ready, and is coached to understand the ramifications of high school and postsecondary choices on further study and work,
  - A climate that encourages each student's voice, and
  - The extra help necessary to succeed and excel at high school.
- Build capacity. Develop a critical mass that is agile enough to be strategic and tactical in managing its own growth and development.
- Be willing to be disturbed. Be prepared for discomfort. Be prepared to deal with it. Do the hard things once.
- Focus on the data and be able to relate data discussions to individual teachers.
- Stay the course; do not be a victim of a carousel of reforms. Stand firm on where you believe your school can go based on the high expectations you set.
- Commit to everything being on the table, from courses to programs to bell schedules to job descriptions.
- Listen to students.
- Have students "build" an ideal teacher, assess in what numbers they exist, and develop a strategy that makes them the norm in your building.
- Use consultants well. Do not use "drive by" strategies. Align the work of consultants. Use them to fan the flames of the fire you set.
- Realize there is no box!

CHAPTER FOUR

Glass Balls and Hedgehogs

T his started out as a chapter on leadership. I was going to extol the virtues and required characteristics of principals and superintendents and set the charge for them to go forth and manage good school reform. But through personal experience and research, I've observed what Michael Fullan states about change. "Change cannot be managed. It can be understood and perhaps led, but it cannot be controlled" (Fullan, 2001, p. 33). Besides, laying the onus for successful reform solely on "designated" leaders defeats the purpose of a redesign and reform movement that is truly in the hands of those closest to the challenge and those who know our students best, classroom teachers and their principals. It in some way devalues the efforts of the group. It also lets most of us off the hook for the results. This is instead, then, a chapter about personal accountability for getting our schools where they need to be.

This change in emphasis was brought home to me by my reading of Stephen R. Covey's *The Eighth Habit: From Effectiveness to Greatness.* In it Covey references a recent Harris poll of 23,000 U.S. residents employed full time in key industries and in key functional areas. The poll found, among other things, that

- Only 37% said they have a clear understanding of what their organization is trying to achieve and why.
- Only one in five was enthusiastic about his or her team's and organization's goals.
- Only one in five workers said he or she has a clear line of sight between his or her tasks and the team's and organization's goals.

- Only half were satisfied with the work they had accomplished at the end of the week.
- Only 15% felt their organization fully enables them to execute key goals.
- Only 15% felt they worked in a high-trust environment.
- Only 17% felt their organization fosters open communication that is respectful of differing opinions and that results in new and better ideas.
- Only 10% felt their organization holds people accountable for results.
- Only 13% have high-trust, highly cooperative working relationships with other groups or departments.

If that isn't startling enough, Covey compares the statistics to a soccer game. He states that only four of the eleven players on the field would know which goal was theirs. Only two of the eleven would care. Only two of the eleven would know what position they play and know exactly what they are supposed to do. And all but two players would, in some way, be competing against their own team members rather than the opponent (Covey, 2004, p. 2). If we can imagine similar statistics from the world of education, is it any wonder that so many of us feel we are on that hamster wheel? It isn't enough simply for the superintendent or principal to understand the "sport" of education. All the players need to know their roles, see the goals, feel impassioned, and know what they are supposed to do if our schools are going to succeed.

So far, we've already looked at the need for a clear mission and vision and for high expectations. We've looked at the power of our data and the need to build capacity. We've realized we can't do this work in isolation and that we need community partners. And we know from the research and best practices that we must expand our thinking about what a high school experience should be for our students and, at the same time, find ways to get small enough to provide individualized learning.

In the rest of this chapter, we will put in place more pieces that create a climate for success as we visit the remaining habits of effective schools: strong, sustained, and shared leadership; effective management and alignment of resources; and understanding time. However, in each instance when we address leadership, I urge you to think about how those characteristics of leaders need to play out at all levels, regardless of anyone's designation as "leader."

Now, imagine a perhaps not-so-mythical district. It is a large- to medium-sized district with multiple high schools. It has a diverse student population in terms of both ethnicity and socioeconomics. It has a consistent track record with national funders. Its test scores and budgets, like those everywhere, are being scrutinized. There is some story in the press that is causing discussion. It has a new, forward-thinking superintendent who is taking steps to realign resources and priorities. There are some new state and federal mandates to consider. Several of the schools have been assigned new principals. The superintendent has announced that a new multipoint plan for getting the system to move forward will be announced shortly. The superintendent asks the leadership to reapply for their jobs. Everyone becomes cautiously optimistic (read this as "simply cautious"). Funders pause in their tracks. The "leadership" becomes hesitant. The work of consultants is on hold. Meetings are cancelled; more meetings are scheduled. Initiatives that were in place are merged, forgotten, or renamed. Teachers in classrooms wonder about the next big thing they will be asked to do. Everyone is holding his or her breath for the dials to be reset, for clarity. The reform work of our mythical district grinds slowly to a stop. Recognize the *"whirr"?* While this reaction might be understandable, it is hardly acceptable as long as we still have thousands of students who deserve an education showing up in our buildings each day.

But regardless of our commitment to students, we are human beings and we know that this is what happens in bureaucratic organizations. As Collins says, "the purpose of bureaucracy is to compensate for incompetence, lack of trust, and lack of discipline" (Collins, 2001, p. 121). The process of reform is not meant to throw out the good work that reaps results for children, or indeed, all the work of the past. If we have the mission right, if we are making decisions based on data and our core values, if we have built the capacity of our educators, and if we are disciplined about our adherence to our plan, the work will continue despite the cycle of change so evident in our school communities. But, too often, we are not there yet. Too many of our schools operate as both bureaucratic and autocratic organizations that have not empowered their staffs, and the hamster wheel cycle of reforms continues.

So how, then, do we manage through the normal life cycle of school systems with a commitment to reforming and redesigning our schools? How do we avoid falling victim to the "stop in your tracks" cycle when a new superintendent, initiative, or principal comes our way? How do we avoid what Fullan calls the "implementation dip"? The period when there "is literally a dip in performance and confidence as one encounters an innovation that requires new skills and understandings." He suggests that when schools are in the dip, the individuals are experiencing both "the psychological fear of change and the lack of technical know-how or skills to make the change work" (Fullan, 2001, pp. 40–41). Knowing the cause provides us with some guidance on how to push past the dip. Designated leaders can put in place supports that help teachers through their fears and design appropriate staff development that bridges a skill gap. In a like manner to the way we turned around the D.U.C.K.S. and F.L.O.C.K.S. discussion in Chapter 3 when we saw an opportunity for building capacity by providing opportunities, creative outlets, knowledge, and skills, we can also address educators' frustration with the bureaucracy they feel too often challenges their success. I have found it a remarkably simple strategy to simply untangle a challenge by looking at the other side of the coin. Look back at the Collins quote, above, on bureaucracy. To begin to break through bureaucratic systems, educators must address these areas, turn them around, and commit to identifying their knowledge gaps and building their competence, building trust, and demonstrating a commitment to disciplined practice.

But, again, if we have done this work well, we will have a groundswell of teachers who have found their voices and demand a reform process that makes sense. They will help steer the ship; they will demand that their voices and the voices of their students are heard. They will state that they "do not want to take it any more." They will have the passion of Howard Beal, and they will not leave each other, or the principal, or the superintendent alone. They will, because they are invested in the work, and have had the hard conversations, and are invested in the process, and realize that they are also accountable. This newly owned accountability must translate into the classroom teachers' commitment to

- Use data to impact instruction,
- Participate in professional learning communities where teachers share their work, practices, student concerns, and professional learning,
- Be in and out of each other's classrooms for the purpose of improving instruction, and
- Reinvent the role of teacher.

They will also be empowered to stand up and ask for the following:

- A coherent set of practices and policies,
- Hiring of new staff, including principals, that is aligned to the mission they have set for the school, and
- School Board representation that understands and supports the work at the school level.

In times of change, if the teachers don't find their voice and the principals don't share their strength, we fall into what I have seen in too many schools: not an implementation dip, but an *implementation crevasse*.

How do we avoid the crevasse? What do we need to get us all going in the right direction? The easy answer would be strong leadership. The more realistic answer is that we all have to be accountable.

If we've done our job right in building capacity, the educators involved have created, *and expect*, a culture that empowers them to lead our schools, which brings us to the glass balls and hedgehogs.

Many years ago when I was attempting to manage multiple contracts, raise kids, grow the company, and write a book, I felt I was juggling too many things and risked dropping the balls. I had a wise mentor then who said "you don't have to keep all the balls in the air at the same time. You just can't drop the glass ones." This simple reflection allowed me to understand that I needed to focus on the key things that would shatter if dropped. I had to ask the hard questions about which balls were rubber and which ones were glass. I had to determine what was "the main thing." Once the glass balls were identified, the rest of the juggling became easier. I could have that laser-like focus on what was essential and not worry if some of the other balls dropped. I had the capacity on my own team to say, "I think this is glass, but if I continue to juggle it it will shatter; you must take care of this one." Over time, in my organization we've narrowed it all down to an uncompromised commitment to reform that leads to high standards and equitable education for all students. We're doing okay if *no one died, no relationships were damaged, and we performed excellently and ethically.*

In schools, most can agree, the glass balls are clearly student academic success, personalized learning communities, professional learning communities, and safety. Yet each of these is undergirded by a complex set of activities and priorities and the fact that our client base changes completely every four years. In high schools we have a unique set of traditions that are set by our own experience, our alumni, and our comfort with past practice. The AP English teacher will always feel that AP English is the distinguishing feature of the high school, and the winning basketball team coach will feel it's basketball. So while we can gain consensus on the big picture, does everyone know which balls are glass? And does everyone agree on what scaffolding of commitment and actions supports a school that holds *the main thing* as the one glass ball that cannot be dropped?

It's Jim Collins's version of the hedgehog approach in *Good to Great*. Collins describes the hedgehog as an animal that goes slowly along, concerned only about taking care of its home and lunch. Hedgehogs do not get distracted by an array of extraneous events or activities. They know what they are about. They don't spend time trying to do things they are not meant to do. They know what they need to do to survive. They stay focused on lunch. That approach is one Collins suggests for organizations and leaders.

> Hedgehogs . . . simplify a complex world into a simple organizing idea, a basic principle or concept that unifies and guides everything. It does not matter how complex the world, a hedgehog reduces all challenges and dilemmas to simple—indeed almost simplistic— hedgehog ideas. For a hedgehog, anything that does not somehow relate to the hedgehog idea holds no relevance. (Collins, 2001, p. 91)

While it may be overly simplistic, for schools to become successful they must reduce their challenges to a hedgehog approach. They must tear through and streamline their ever-competing and demanding priorities into a seamless plan to meet their goal of a highly personalized environment for learning and leading. Leadership, of course, is critical. Fullan says it well:

> Leadership is to the current decade what the standards movement was to the 1990s. Standards, even when well implemented, can take us only part way to successful large-scale reform. It is only leadership that can take us all the way. (Fullan, 2003, p. 16)

The need for school leadership is increasingly noted in the literature.

> As schools experience new pressures from every quarter, the challenges of leading them toward meaningful improvement has never loomed larger. As (Essential) schools face the task of restructuring their entire institutional culture, the principal still acts as the fulcrum of school leadership. But given these daunting new circumstances, schools now need every leader they can get. (Coalition of Essential Schools National Office, n.d.)

We all must be leaders.

Let's address some of the traits identified for good leaders. Let us also, for now, agree that those "designated as leaders" are the ones who need to have these traits in order to ensure that their organizations succeed. In workshops, the educators I work with frequently generate lists of leader characteristics that include the words charismatic, strong, driven, decisive, consistent, and fair. In a recent workshop in Houston, Texas, one educator said, "All those things are fine, but isn't it also important that they know something?" Amid the laughter, we also quickly added "informed, knowledgeable, and with evidence of content mastery" to our desired leadership characteristics. Missing from the list was any reference to leaders needing to know how to get results. You might be surprised at how rarely "helps us meet our benchmarks or goals" ever makes it to the character trait list.

Useful resources on leadership criteria expand the desired characteristics noted above. "A leader is someone who sets direction, demonstrates personal character, builds organizational capacity, and mobilizes individual commitments" (Ten³ Business E-Coach, n.d.). A recent American Airlines *American Way* magazine article described an effective leader as humble, inclusive, broad-minded, intimate, values oriented, empathetic, and absolutely honest (McGarvey, 2004, pp. 24–26). Collins (2001), in looking at top-performing leaders, those he identifies as "Level Five" leaders, notes they have similar traits. They are humble and demonstrate a strong professional will. They set their successors up for success. They have compelling modesty. They are frenetically driven to do what must be done for results, and they are willing to make the hard decisions. They are more of a plow horse (working) than a show horse (taking the credit and being out and about). When things are going poorly they hold a mirror to themselves; when things are going well they look out their office window to the people who make the organization work (pp. 22–39).

We know what we want from leaders, but what do we want them to "do," and how do we measure their capability to meet their mission?

> The easy answer is (in) getting people to do things they have never thought of doing, do not believe possible, and do not want to do. The organizational answer is the action of committing employees to contribute their best to the purpose of the organization. The complex (and more accurate) answer is you only know leadership by its consequences—from the fact that individuals in a group of people start to behave in a particular way as results of the actions of someone else. (Ten³ Business E-Coach, n.d.)

It's the fourth "R" in the often-discussed *rigor, relevance, and relationships* approach to school reform. It's about getting *results*. Now let's relate all those leadership traits and results back to the multiple tiers of individuals who work with and in our schools. Is there anything on any of the lists that we should not *expect* from every superintendent, director, principal, or classroom teacher? Of course not! We would be elated if all children could develop the literacy and numeracy skills they have never thought of acquiring, do not believe they can achieve, and (in many cases) do not want to acquire. This look at leadership, then, requires that we understand that depending on the situation, each of us serves a different role as a strategic, operational, or team leader. Once we begin to understand this, we can take ownership of the situation and hold our colleagues and ourselves accountable for our success.

Traditionally, strategic leaders have responsibility for the whole organization. Operational leaders have responsibility for one segment of the organization, and team leaders guide a specific task, action, or committee. But in schools, especially, these are fluid leadership roles. The building principal is a strategic leader in his or her own building, but when involved in the district's principal leadership circle, for example, his or her role changes. Department chairs are operational leaders until they go to their district-level meetings where the district department chair serves as the operational leader. Teachers are the strategic leaders of their classrooms, yet they may head a school-based committee and thus serve as a team leader, and so on. In a climate that increasingly demands new roles and shared responsibilities, the same high expectations for leadership and accountability for keeping the glass balls in the air should be shared by all in the building.

This commitment to strong, shared, and sustained leadership, our fifth habit of highly effective schools, requires the development of new ways of operating. Educators must move away from dependency on others as they build their own capacity to succeed at reform.

> First, many teachers and principals may have developed a fostered dependency from the prescription period, and when invited to engage in informed professional judgment, they may respond by saying, "Tell us what to do." Second, it takes capacity to build capacity, hence teachers and principals who have not worked together this way before may not know what to do. (Fullan, 2003, p. 26)

The hard conversations we referenced in Chapter 3 go a long way to getting organizations to the point where they have a shared vision and mission. We don't want compliance from our educators; we want commitment. It is hoped these hard conversations have set the tone and readiness for shared ownership of the reform and redesign work. Undoubtedly, however, given our understanding of a nonlinear approach to all of this work, we need to go back and review roles and responsibilities as we currently perceive them, throw the job description on the table, and see what currently makes sense. Even if you did this early on in the redesign process, the changes your organization has experienced will warrant a review. The MetLife Survey of the American Teacher (MetLife, 2003) is a remarkably helpful tool here for looking at the disconnects between the role of the principal and the perception of that role by teachers, students, and parents. Don't be misled into thinking that it is only the principal's job that will need scrutiny; it is the job of everyone in the process. The MetLife survey is important because it brings to the fore the need to communicate the changing roles and responsibilities to the community.

In the developmental process of redesigning our schools, and with the understanding that it indeed takes time to grow a new culture, we can only hope that at the state and district levels, consistency of practice supports redesign work. However, as I said earlier, we're not there yet. Across the country, for example, we are woefully inconsistent at establishing policies that support our mission statements. Most states, for example, have policies that allow students to drop out of school or seek a GED once they reach the age of 16. This flies in the face of good educational practice, high expectations, and what we know students will need to know and be able to do as they transition from student to independent young adult to adult. While we wait for state and federal policies to catch up with a changing set of expectations, it frequently falls to the building-level principal to provide the leadership to nurture the reforms. A few forward-thinking districts have had the foresight to add a "school improvement facilitator" or "reform coordinator" as the in-house person designated to co-lead the reform with the principal. While not yet commonplace, the addition of this person establishes the importance of a focus on reform for each school. Since this is a new position for schools, there is often a fine dance that has to be undertaken as principal and coordinator work out a balance between their roles and responsibilities in a changing school.

Undoubtedly, these individuals are already tasked with taking the lead on much of the work that we addressed in Chapter 3. In addition, they, along with an empowered school leadership team, have created the context for the work around the broader vision for shared leadership described in this chapter. Perhaps their next big task, then, is to address the last two habits of effective schools: effective management and alignment of resources, and understanding time.

Last year, in the midst of my own personal struggle with getting past the hamster wheel phenomenon, I did a three-day professional development session with a large southern school system. One of our tasks was to begin to align their work with their mission. As a start, we asked the participants to bring in their district school improvement plans and any other planning documents for grants, professional development, budgets, and the like. There was sheer horror on the faces of the participants as they reviewed the documents. There was no "main thing." Each document reflected the hand of different authors despite the fact that they were frequently cut and pasted from each other. They lacked coherency and none of them reflected the same priorities or goals for the school. In some, literacy was paramount, in others the goal was safety, still another quoted verbatim the district goals for students adding no personalized learning signature for this uniquely positioned school. In addition, the budgets and the availability of federal program support were not being used to support key initiatives. Indeed, several of the schools were able to hold up three different plans for the same year, each of which captured a set of three sometimes-competing priorities. When we began to look at the business partnerships, resources, and use of professional development time, we again were able to see a disconnect between what the schools stated as their goals and how they were using resources. I could hear the *whirring* in my head and the sense of tension growing in me and in the participating educators. We were paralyzed in a maze of reform initiatives and competing plans.

A simple process, however, of beginning to recommit to the mission and then literally charting out the top priorities that supported the mission resulted in a chart that allowed us to see where the connections and the disconnections were in school operations. We were able to ask more probing questions about why staff development was disconnected from meeting specific goals, how we could better utilize the federal dollar allocations to support the mission, and how we could use consultants to support schools. Ultimately, we were able to straighten the maze, so to speak. We matched resources to priorities, identified key personnel to address the issues, and set reasonable timelines to carry out our now-streamlined and aligned priorities. Equally important, we began to identify some of the stressors that call for multiple plans to be written. This process took three days, time we don't always have or take in schools to get it right.

Our last habit for schools is understanding time. That which we have so little of is the thing that we have to manage best. It will always be easiest, especially in schools, to be distracted. There is the child in crisis, the child to celebrate, the parent who needs you, the business partner, the superintendent, the classroom to visit, the report to write, the sporting event to attend, the special education issue to address, the discussions with lawyers, the grievance to deal with, the union meeting, grades to get in, back to school night, publications review, the department meeting, the technology meeting, the alumni, the facilities meeting, the budget, and so on. At all levels of leadership (please read this to mean everyone working with schools), it is imperative that we begin to make sense out of the time we have and establish the practices of time and priority management that support success. One principal I work with indicated how important it was to her to have an "open door policy" in order to be accessible to her staff. When she realized that she was getting less and less work done as staff continued to drop by, she revised her policy. She continues to have an open door policy. Her door is open from 7:00–7:45 A.M. daily and from 3:10–4:30 P.M. three days a week. At all other times you need an appointment. The result of her decision was that the staff had to manage their time so that they were ready for meetings with her, and as a result everyone became more productive. As the school got better at looking at time, they streamlined meetings, holding them only when it was important to bring the faculty together. This required a commitment by the faculty to read e-mail and other communications, and an understanding that if they didn't take responsibility for that they may indeed be "out of the loop." Managing and respecting time is part of the culture shift, and culture, as one management specialist said, is what keeps the herd roughly moving west.

The ongoing commitment to the culture shift requires all the leadership traits mentioned above and some specific additional skills. Strong leaders need to

- Understand and assess their own strengths, weaknesses, and professional development needs as they relate to the reform,
- Look at their staffs and ask the hard questions about their strengths, weaknesses, and professional development gaps,
- Establish a compelling reason why reform and redesign are critically important,
- Engage and ignite the community's passion for successful students and excellence in teaching,
- Understand that confusion can paralyze a team and that people do their best work when the goals and expectations are clear,
- Hold hard and honest conversations about the direction of the school because without these hard conversations they will ultimately return to square one in the design process,
- Engage all stakeholders and bridge the engagement gap by letting each person see the importance of his or her involvement in the process,

- Take the pulse of the school community and assess the level of readiness and involvement through such informal measures as community forums and one-on-one conversations and the more data-driven measures of low teacher attendance rates, poor participation at faculty meetings, and a set of stalled improvement strategies,
- Hold policy conversation both up and down the chain of command, and push to align those policies with the mission of the school,
- Minimize the disconnects between policy and practice,
- Realize that there are things that they can and cannot control and that they must make sense of that for their faculty,
- Enact new policies that make sense and are coherent with the mission,
- Work to avoid "episodic improvement" and short-term gains, and keep an eye on the ultimate goal for their redesigned school,
- Make hard decisions and put the right people in the tough spots, and put the best resources where they are most needed,
- Model what they expect from others,
- Set the context for the learning and unsettle people in ways that support the reform,
- Build a team that can own the redesign and develop a structure that supports their work,
- Take responsibility for developing the leadership in staff for multiple roles, including their own replacement,
- Document successes and failures and understand that failure is an opportunity for new learning,
- Communicate continually,
- Find meaningful ways to celebrate success and motivate staff, and
- Realize that there is a cycle to reform. There will be dips, new staff, new families, changed policies, and new challenges, and this means that much of the work has to be redone, honed, and reexamined regularly.

My colleague, Dr. Deborah Wortham, director of professional development for Baltimore City Public Schools, has a simple and helpful formula for success:

- Clarify beliefs first. Yours and theirs. Reach consensus.
- Hold meaningful faculty meetings—use time, professional development, and professional learning communities for furthering the work.

- Review the data and be *restless* about the pace of improvement. Act immediately.
- Celebrate success and cultivate individual leadership qualities.

If you do all this, how will you know whether you are successful? How will you know whether you've established a culture that is virtually immune from the hamster wheel phenomenon? You will know when it is clear that in your building, and in each building in the district, teacher quality is the dominant indicator of success and each student is welcomed, respected, and has high expectations. You will know it's real when the policies and practices are aligned to keep the glass balls in the air, and the hedgehogs are so effectively engaged in setting the standard for success that you cannot, nor would you want to, wrestle it away from them.

> *Groups want someone to have authority, sometimes even to make them do things they don't feel like doing. We all need to be pushed, but not shoved—the balancing act every teacher knows and grapples with.*
>
> —Coalition of Essential
> Schools National Office, n.d.

Glass Balls and Hedgehogs

- Know what "the main thing" is.
- Be able to identify the glass balls.
- Keep a laser-like, hedgehog focus on the main thing.
- Realize that there may be an implementation dip and use Fullan's strategy of addressing the psychological fear of change and providing technical knowledge and skills to staff.
- Don't let the implementation dip become an implementation crevasse.
- Attack Collins's explanation for the need for bureaucracies by committing to filling the knowledge gaps, creating competence, building trust, and committing to disciplined practice.
- Teachers must commit to
  - o Use data to impact instruction,
  - o Participate in professional learning communities where teachers share their work, practices, student concerns, and professional learning,
  - o Be in and out of each other's classrooms for the purpose of improving instruction, and
  - o Reinvent the role of teacher.
- Educators must demand
  - o A coherent set of practices and policies,
  - o Hiring of new staff, including principals, that are aligned to the mission they have set for the school, and
  - o School Board representation that understands and supports the work at the school level.
- Get out your school plans and documents and assess whether they are aligned.
- Tear through and streamline your ever-competing and demanding priorities into a seamless plan to meet your goal of a highly personalized environment for learning and leading.
- Understand we all must be leaders.

CHAPTER FIVE

The Simple Truth

W e've undertaken quite a journey in this book, accompanied by hamsters, skunks, ducks, elephants, and hedgehogs. And while the Noah's Ark of characters provides humor and focus, the hard work is still to be done. We've taken a hard look at schools. In some cases the examples were probably too close for comfort, but that's the honest part of this work. It's hard, ongoing, developmental, and it only really works if you are willing to speak truthfully about your successes and failures. And the simple truth is that all the effort surrounding reform has not yet led to the success we want for schools and students. We've just begun the journey.

As Fullan suggests, "the examples we have looked at are not really examples of transformation but rather preliminary baby steps [that] reveal how deep the necessary cultural change really is" (Fullan, 2001, p. 70). The baby steps must stride more forcefully into accountable work habits if we are going to leave a positive footprint on the schools we serve.

While outlining this chapter, I was listening to Ronald Reagan's funeral service. I could not help but thank Margaret Thatcher for so concisely summarizing the steps we need to follow to leave that footprint. She unwittingly laid out what we need to do to find the mettle for the balance of our work. In describing what she believed was the essence of Reagan's success, Lady Thatcher stated,

- He knew what he wanted.
- He acted decisively.
- He acknowledged his and others' roles as leaders.
- He had resolve and was unyielding in staying focused on the mission.

- He never shrank from a task.
- He developed strategies to carry everyone with him.
- And he knew, always, what he and America stood for.

That, in short, is the simple truth of this reform work. We strive to create schools of excellence. The leadership perceived in Reagan by Lady Thatcher shows us how. At the end of the day, we must ensure that these truths spread to *each* of our classrooms. In the early stages of the reform work we believed that by simply creating small learning communities, we would see positive changes in instruction, the development of a shared professional community, and a standard of high expectations for *all* students. Now we know we must begin with an essential question that fundamentally challenges our approach to how we teach and how we manage schools. The magic wand I carry in my briefcase really doesn't work. We have to take the time to get the right people, in the right jobs, with a shared commitment to high expectations. We must have a clear vision of how we are going to get there and establish the policies and practices that result in good teaching.

Good teaching matters. The 1987 Mortimer and Sammons study showed that the impact of *good* teaching has between six and ten times more impact on learning *than all other home and environmental factors combined* (Mortimer & Sammons, 1987, pp. 4–8). While that study focused on students in elementary schools, we now have convergent research from Johns Hopkins. Additional research indicates that consistent and effective teaching for a *consecutive series of two to four years* can turn around underperforming students at the high school level.

Part of effective teaching, of course, comes from listening to the voice of the students. In Chapter 3, we heard echoes from student focus groups from across the country. We heard their perspective on good teaching and their desire for respect. We watched them "build their ideal teacher." It is the voices of the students that require us to create an environment in which *all* students thrive as creative learners. These are the voices that demand adjustments in how and what we teach. It is sometimes uncomfortable for us, as adults, to reflect that it is the students, and the world they are preparing for, that must drive our work. We must remember that it is not our love of the subject matter, or of a particular lesson, or certainly of a "bump" in the state test scores that drives good teaching. It is, however, for the love of teaching students to learn that I believe we are drawn to education. It is my hope that it is their voices that motivate us, each day, to stay in the classroom or to serve as instructional coaches, or administrators, or guidance counselors, or school board representatives. It is this love and commitment that must also drive us to create policies that make school work for students. There is a societal motivation, of course; the students of today will be the ones caring for us and for society as we age. But there is something about the magic of teaching and students that keeps us in the game. We know that we learn as much from our students as we teach them.

I had a wonderful reminder of this while working, again, in Junction City, Kansas. Principal Springston was hosting a faculty barbeque. I was talking to my now-favorite educator and theorist, Eric. At the time of my visit, he was seven years old. In the inane conversations that adults so often have with young children, I asked him such brilliant questions as "What grade are you in?" "Do you like school?" and "What is your favorite subject?" I was impressed when Eric told me that his favorite subject was math. I applauded Eric's love for math and confessed my own challenges with the subject. I was not prepared for what came next. Eric was simply astonished that anyone could not understand and not love math. He borrowed a pen from his dad, escorted me to the buffet table, and grabbed a paper plate. He firmly announced that we were going to do math, that I would understand it, and that we were going to start with "In and Out Boxes." I knew I was in trouble; not even in "the new math" of my grade school years did we have in and out boxes. He flipped over the plate and drew what you see below.

Eric enthusiastically explained that we had to figure out just two things. "First," he said, "look at the in and out boxes. If we see a '3' in the first 'in box' and a '15' in the first 'out box,' we have to figure out what we should see in the other 'out boxes' across from the two and the five. Secondly," he continued, "we have to figure out what 'rule' makes this happen." Thinking I understood, and feeling confident in my five-times table, I got brave. Grateful that he had picked multiplications of five, not eight, I guessed that the second out box should have a 10 in it and that the third out box should have a 25 in it. Eric said, "I think you are probably right, but why?" I told him that my hypothesis was that the "rule" was the five-times table. "If that's right," he went on, "what should be in the fourth in box?" I suggested that this, indeed, seemed to be changing things. I felt like now I was being asked to do division and that didn't seem quite fair, but I guessed "6," and Eric applauded my efforts. Then, however, he asked me to prove my guess by coming up with three examples of my own by using the lower set of in and out boxes. Here's what my completed plate looked like.

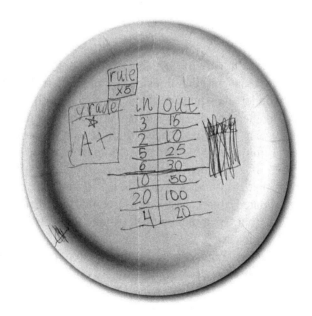

Eric awarded me my first, and only, A+ in math. He proudly placed that mark in, of course, the "grade box." I had such a sense of accomplishment! But seven-year-old Eric was not about to let me stop there. He challenged me to do more as he deftly grabbed another plate from the buffet table and created my next assignment. You see it on the next page.

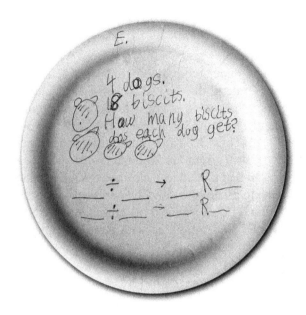

Sad to say, I was horrified. "If there are four dogs, and you have 18 dog biscuits, how many biscuits does each dog get?" Although Eric had put together a wonderful display, demonstrating the multiple intelligences of his artistic, mathematical, and English skills, he couldn't disguise it from me. This was a "math challenged" individual's worst nightmare—*a word problem*! I immediately saw that problem from my own youth flash before my eyes: "If a train leaves the station at 1:00. . . ." What made it even worse was that Eric said he expected me to find *two* answers. I told Eric I was intimidated, that I wasn't sure I could do it. Eric calmly said, "No problem. See that 'E' at the top of the plate? It stands for *example,* so it's okay if you get it wrong."

So, after using my fingers and toes, the calculator on my cell phone, and a little help from Eric, I solved it. Here are our results.

Eric was a great teacher! For me, the wonder of this story is threefold. I learned that math could be fun and that I didn't have to be intimidated—okay, maybe only slightly intimidated. I learned the magic of good teaching; surely Eric was mirroring the way his own teachers taught him. And lastly, I learned how educational theory and practices are truly formed. Remember the "grade box" I referred to earlier? I asked Eric about that. He said, "I just made that up; it makes sense."

In Frederick Hess's article *Tough Love for School Reform,* he states, "Educational reformers routinely approach school improvement as a matter of technical expertise rather than common sense—undermining their own best efforts while distracting public attention and energy from the larger structural problems" (Hess, 2004, p. 1).

While I concur with Hess, it gets back to the question of *why,* when we know what we want to create for our schools, is it so difficult to create that climate for success? As we have already seen, rarely is it a lack of commitment to children. Often, it is not having the skills to understand and implement change. Sometimes it is not having the plan, and sometimes it is simply about not having the mettle to go where our minds and hearts tell us we should. But like Eric and the grade box, and as Hess suggests, *we need to do what makes sense.* The simple truth is that effective high schools make sense for kids. But as Silva and Mackin point out in their work, "making sense for kids, however, often drives us crazy" (Silva & Mackin, 2002, p. 65).

The stories I have shared in this book are all true. While they may have been too close to home, I hope they have disturbed you in the direction of committing and recommitting to creating a good high school. Each story is a real-life lesson from the field, from the educators both young and "seasoned" who are doing the work. In the telling, I hope I have created a vehicle for educators to be open to those opportunities and individuals that teach us about a commitment to continuous improvement. School reform is about creating in each of us, and in our students, the desire to constantly know, observe, and learn. It is about nurturing *all* students to high expectations so that when they leave high school they are what *Raising Our Sights: No High School Senior Left Behind* calls "ready and eager to learn more" (National Commission on the Senior Year, 2001, p. 9).

Battling the hamster wheel isn't easy. In truth, there have been many times since that meeting back in Maryland with that dedicated faculty that I was not sure there was an answer to getting off the wheel—or any way to effectively write about it. Like many of the schools I was serving, I remained stuck, running in place, for quite awhile. *Whirr.*

I found I agreed with the *Miami Herald* reporter Rosebeth Moss Kantor in her assessment of public education. "The pathetic pace of change in public education," she stated, "is sometimes blamed, unfairly, on educators. But like book-deprived children, educators themselves often lack tools—especially tools for making necessary changes" (Kantor, 2004).

I was feeling very frustrated at the "pathetic pace." How could I continue to work with schools if I believed in the hamster wheel? *Whirr.*

Then I had the wonderful opportunity to fall asleep in my parents' home and dream. I dreamt that I was called in to be a substitute teacher. Okay, so the dream actually begins as a nightmare! I arrived at the school and I found out that I was to be a long-term "sub" in, of all subjects, *Algebra I.* I was asked to take the "repeater" class. As so often happens in my educational career, I knew I was in trouble.

I arrived in my classroom. Because these were the repeaters, you know that it was a classroom in a corner of the building, cut off from other students so that they wouldn't cross-pollinate with or contaminate the *good* students. My class roster of 35 was reflected in a classroom of 17 students. The room itself was a terrible "L" shaped room, with students seated in a scatter pattern.

While I knew my algebraic skills were lacking, I also knew that getting all the kids at least on one side of the room was important for classroom management. I asked them to move to one side of the room. And, *because after all it was a dream*, they happily complied with my request.

I said, in English, to my mixed lingual students, "I am glad you are here. Where is everyone else?" They seemed confused by such a simple question. It seems no one had ever bothered to ask. I told them I needed to share a few things:

- I'd be honest with them.
- I'd respect them.
- I was not a master of the subject matter, but together we would succeed.
- I knew they each knew something that they could share and teach. They had failed algebra. *They had not failed life.*

I told them,

- It wasn't going to be easy and there would be tests.
- Failure was not an option. There was *no way* we were going to try this together again!
- Humor would be important.
- They would have homework, but it would be reasonable.

For homework the first day, I gave an assignment. The next day they were to bring to class one person who was assigned to this class and who was not attending. And, *because after all it was still a dream*, they did.

At the close of day two, I had a full class. And, because it was a dream, I had mastered the skills I needed to teach algebra and I had met my personal improvement goal that I shared in Chapter 3: *I could speak Spanish!* As the bell rang, I stood at the door and said to *each* student, "Thank you for being here. I missed some of you yesterday. We all need to be together tomorrow."

It was that simple sentence that, when I awoke, gave me the hope to write this book and get back in the trenches. Getting it right in schools, *in each classroom*, is as simple as accepting where we are and welcoming everyone into the process so that they are both supported and held accountable. Getting it right means recognizing that we all have to be together tomorrow.

I used to feel guilty about getting angry and frustrated about this work we call high school reform. In an effort to get "unstuck," I consulted my colleagues from across the country and from across reform initiatives. I asked them to point me to a high school that had really attained *and maintained* success for *all* students. While we collectively were able to generate lists of schools in which the 9th-grade advisory was working well; or the district was asking the right questions; or there was a good senior project or literacy program; or places were being creative with administrative, department, and guidance structures; or schools were seeing academic gains for some of their students, we could not come up with a list of schools that had completely succeeded. We noted the excellent resources that High Schools That Work documents with their "pacesetter" sites, and the Northwest Regional Education Lab's Web site displays smaller learning communities schools making progress. In addition, NASSP has noted "Break Through Schools"; the Education Trust has research on the remarkable gains made by some 90-90-90 schools (those with student populations consisting of 90% minorities with 90% of the student body on free and reduced lunch and with a 90% success rate on state tests); and the U.S. Department of Education's old New American High School program provides some good examples. However, not one of my colleagues could point to a single school where they thought all the elements of a good high school were in place. In fact, we all added caveats to our recommendations that suggested we were unsure of the stability of gains made. "You should probably check to see if this is still true; they just got a new principal (or superintendent)," "The bond issue didn't pass," or "Their grant funds ran out last year" were frequent add-ons to our recommendations.

The fact that many schools are not succeeding undoubtedly opens the door for a further debate about small schools vs. smaller learning communities vs. schools that are redesigned, reinvented, and reconfigured. It gets us back to an essential question: how do we define an effective school, and how do we know it when we see it?

Naïvely, I wanted to conclude *Hamster Wheel* with just the right answers and no more questions. I felt, in the final writing of this, that I should be able to wrap that question up for the reader, ignoring my own statement in Chapters 2 and 3 that it is those closest to the challenge who have the best solutions. With that, I had the good fortune of referring back to Robert Eaker and Richard and Rebecca DuFour's book *Getting Started: Reculturing Schools to Become Professional Learning Communities.* In addition to the excellent strategies in the book, there was also a reference to Victor Frankel's 1959 work on human nature. In *Man's Search for Meaning,* Frankel avows that our most basic human need is to feel a sense of accomplishment.

Refer back to the list presented in Chapter 2 that itemized indicators of possible hamster wheel phenomena. Imagine if the list was reversed and your school now had all goals aligned, policies supported creativity and risk, meetings were effective, students and teachers felt valued, all students were succeeding, and the movie was not *Groundhog Day* but *The Greatest Story Ever Told*. It could be the story of your school or district. Then educators would have a passion for their work as they operated in a system that sets a standard for excellence. The sense of good work alone would help move the school forward. Reform work, when done in a positive climate, provides a meaningful life for those engaged in the process. I said it in Chapter 2: I just want to celebrate success. Isn't that what we all want in our schools?

Gandhi is credited with saying, "You must be the change you want to see in the world." I suggest, however, that we cannot be that change if we are in the midst of Arnold Fege's "innovation fatigue." We must find ways to build professional community and to focus on the simple truths of organizational change, leadership, and the creation of a climate for success. We must listen for the *whirr* of the hamster wheel and stop it. We must find ways in our experience with schools to

- Rest,
- Read,
- Rebuild,
- Refresh, and
- Recharge.

Then we can reform, reinvent, reconfigure, and commit to continuous improvement. And only then can we, together, hop off, stay off, and drag others off the hamster wheel.

Gracias por estar aquí. Extrañe a unos de ustedes ayer. Todos de nosotros necesitamos estar juntos mañana.

—Thank you for being here.
I missed some of you yesterday.
We all need to be together tomorrow.

Battling the Hamster Wheel Strategies

- Understand that regardless of the moniker—changing, reforming, redesigning, reinventing, reconfiguring, converting, transforming, or obliterating the American high school—it is, at the core, about realizing that our schools, as they currently exist, do not meet the needs of nor set high expectations necessary for our students.
- Commit to continuous improvement.
- Honor the simple truth of this work: effective high schools must make sense for students.
- Have hard conversations; ask hard questions.
- Keep the skunk on the table.
- Know your data.
- Ensure that your mission statement is "the main thing."
- Enact the habits of highly effective schools: demonstrate high expectations and a vision that matches them; build capacity and create a true climate for success; think small and dream big; engage in legitimate community support; thrive with strong, sustained, and shared leadership; effectively align and manage resources; understand time.
- Make it about the students: respecting them, their success, their voice, and their *authentic* involvement in instruction, assessment, and decisions.
- Create a sense of urgency.
- Understand that everything is on the table.
- Keep the glass balls in the air.
- Remember the WIFMs. Include everyone in the process, help them to see their place in the process, and coach them to success.
- Understand that leadership matters. Create a solid leadership team that is *really* empowered to grow a school to greatness.
- Set a meaningful agenda (read this as "school improvement plan") that is achievable and aligned to the main thing and is known by all stakeholders.
- Communicate, communicate, and communicate. Then, communicate, check for understanding, and seek feedback.
- Know the ties that bind. Be clear about barriers, parameters, and limitations to either individual roles or implementation outcomes.
- Make hard decisions.
- Hire well.
- Remember to laugh.
- Risk success; create a high-standards environment for teaching and learning.
- Don't wait to make changes. Make progress not excuses. Success leads to success. Mistakes when dealt with honestly and openly are a chance to learn more.
- Dare to dream a school that doesn't yet exist for your students!
- Battle the hamster wheel.
- Win.

References

Allen, R. (2004, August). Making high schools better. *Education Update, 46*(5). Retrieved August 19, 2004, from www.ascd.org

America's Choice. (n.d.). Retrieved from www.ncee.org/acsd

ASCD Smartbrief. (n.d.). Retrieved from www.smartbrief.com/ascd/

Balfanz, R., & Legters, N. (2004, June). *Locating the dropout crisis.* Baltimore: Johns Hopkins University, Center for Social Organization of Schools.

Bay Area Coalition for Equitable Schools. (n.d.). Retrieved from www.bayces.org

Bryant, W., & Liu, B. (2003, July 21). School day doldrums. *USA Today,* p. 1.

Career Academy Support Network. (n.d.). Retrieved from www.casn-berkeley.edu

Coalition of Essential Schools National Office. (n.d.). Retrieved from www .essentialschools.org

Collins, J. (2001). *Good to great: Why some companies make the leap . . . and others don't.* New York: Harper Business.

Connors, N. A. (2000). *If you don't feed the teachers they eat the students: Guide to success for administrators and teachers.* Nashville, TN: Incentive.

Cottrell, D. (2002). *Monday morning leadership.* Dallas, TX: Cornerstone Leadership Institute.

Covey, S. R. (2004). *The 8th habit: From effectiveness to greatness.* New York: Free Press.

Daggett's nine characteristics of successful schools. (2004). Retrieved October, 2004, from www.daggett.com/PP/9Characteristics.ppt

Darling-Hammond, L. (1997). *The right to learn: A blueprint for creating schools that work.* San Francisco: Jossey-Bass.

Dell'Angela, T. (2004, September 24). New small schools feel pains of change. *Chicago Tribune,* p. 1.

Eaker, R., DuFour, R., & DuFour, R. (2002). *Getting started: Reculturing schools to become professional learning communities.* Bloomington, IN: National Education Service.

The Education Trust. (n.d.). Retrieved from www2.edtrust.org

Elliot, M., Gilroy, C., & Hanser, L. (2002). Career academies: Additional evidence of positive student outcomes. *Journal of Education for Students Placed at Risk, 7*(1), 71–90.

Fege, A. F. (2004, May 18). Schools embrace innovation. *USA Today,* p. A20.

First Things First. (n.d.). Retrieved from www.irre.org/ftf/

Fullan, M. (2001). *Leading in a culture of change.* San Francisco: Jossey-Bass.

Fullan, M. (2003). *The moral imperative of school leadership.* Thousand Oaks, CA: Corwin Press.

Gladwell, M. (2002). *The tipping point: How little things can make a big difference.* Boston: Back Bay Books.

GMS Partners, Inc. (n.d.). Retrieved from www.gmspartnersinc.org

Hess, F. M. (2004). *Tough love for school reform.* San Francisco: WestEd.

High Schools That Work. (n.d.). Retrieved from www.sreb.org/programs/hstw/ hstwindex.asp

Kantor, R. M. (2004, August 26). School reform elusive without ample resources. *Miami Herald.* Retrieved August, 2004 from www.miami.com/mld/ miamiherald

Kelleher, P., & Levenson, M. R. (2004). Can school culture change? *The School Administrator Web Edition.* Retrieved September 21, 2004, from www.aasa .org/publications/sa/2004_09/colkelleher.htm

The Knowledge Loom. (n.d.). Retrieved from www.knowledgeloom.org

Le Segretain, P. (2003, June 8). As diplomat, Bush scores. *USA Today.* Retrieved June, 2003, from www.usatoday.com/news/washington/2003-06-08-bush-trip_x.htm

Maney, K. (2004, July 21). CEO Ollila says Nokia's "sisu" will see it past tough times; Company banks on its "guts," 140-year history to rebound. *USA Today,* p. B01.

McBride, W. (1997). *Entertaining an elephant: A novel about learning and letting go.* San Francisco: Pearl Street Press.

McGarvey, R. (2004, September 15). Field guide to the new CEO. *American Way Magazine,* 24–26.

MetLife. (2003). *The MetLife survey of the American teacher: An examination of school leadership.* Retrieved September 13, 2005, from www.metlife.com/ WPSAssets/20781259951075837470V1F2003%20Survey.pdf

Mid-Continent Regional Educational Laboratory. (n.d.). Retrieved from www.mcrel.org

Mortimer, P., & Sammons, P. (1987). New evidence on effective elementary schools. *Educational Leadership, 45,* 4–8.

National Academy Foundation. (n.d.). Retrieved from www.naf.org

National Association of Secondary School Principals. (1996). *Breaking ranks: Changing an American institution.* Reston, VA: Author.

National Association of Secondary School Principals (Ed.). (2004). *Breaking ranks II: Strategies for leading high school reform.* Reston, VA: Author.

National Commission on Excellence in Education. (1983). *A nation at risk.* Washington, DC: U.S. Government Printing Office.

National Commission on the Senior Year. (2001). *Raising our sights: No high school senior left behind.* Princeton, NJ: The Woodrow Wilson National Fellowship Foundation.

National Commission on Teaching and America's Future. (1996). *What matters most: Teaching and America's future.* New York: Author.

National High School Alliance. (n.d.). Retrieved from www.hsalliance.org

National Right to Read Foundation. (2003). *Paige blasts "soft bigotry of low expectations"* [Press Release]. Manassas Park, VA: Author.

North Central Regional Educational Laboratory. (n.d.). Retrieved from www.ncrel.org

Northwest Regional Education Laboratory. (n.d.). Retrieved from www.nwrel.org

Public Education Network Weekly Newsblast. (n.d.). Retrieved from www.publiceducation.org

Sammon, G. (2000). *Creating and sustaining small learning communities: A practitioner's guide and CD-ROM tool kit for career academies and other small learning communities.* Silver Spring, MD: Upstream Press.

Silva, P., & Mackin, R. (2002). *Standards of mind and heart: Creating the good high school.* New York: Teachers College Press.

Slavin, R. (1997, April). *Sand, bricks, and seeds: School change strategies and readiness for reform.* Baltimore: Johns Hopkins University, Center for Social Organization of Schools.

Talent Development High Schools. (n.d.). Retrieved from www.csos.jhu.edu/tdhs/

Ten³ Business E-Coach. (n.d.). Retrieved May, 2004, from www.1000ventures.com

Toch, T. (2003). *High schools on a human scale: How small schools can transform American education.* Boston: Beacon Press.

Wagner, T. (2003). *Making the grade: Reinventing America's schools.* New York: Falmer Press.

Wheatley, M. (2002). *Turning to one another: Simple conversations to restore hope to the future.* San Francisco: Berrett-Koehler.

Index

Book Study and Facilitation Guide

> Far and away the best prize that life offers is the chance to work hard at work worth doing.
>
> —*Theodore Roosevelt*

Thank you for engaging in *Battling the Hamster Wheel*™. If you've made your way to this section of the manuscript you know that reading the text is just the beginning. Whether you are working through this section on your own, with a group of colleagues, or as the leader of a study or reform group you'll find that this section will refer to key elements of the text. It can be used either before or after you read each section—either to bring enhanced purpose to your reading or to deepen your reflection. Regardless of your point of entry, this study guide asks you to place your experience, your goals, your reform effort, and your own skunks on the table. It asks that you plan to silence the *whirr*.

This guide is meant for

- Principals,
- Teachers,
- School improvement teams,
- School improvement or change facilitators,
- District staff,
- School boards,
- Local Education Funds,
- Business and community partners,
- Administrative leadership networks,
- College and university education classes,

- Consultants who work with schools, and
- Individuals who care about the state of high schools.

Throughout the process of writing *Hamster Wheel,* I continued to work with schools; I realized that the schools most serious about reform were the ones that continually pushed the envelope, were restless for their own success, and continued to ask deep questions. These are the schools that most often have established true professional learning communities or utilized the effective strategies of Critical Friends Groups (CFGs). Often, they were the ones with designated "change agents."

I am always amazed at and grateful for our collective learning through questioning. In addition to the "Junction City questions" noted in Chapter 2, there have been three sets of questions or reflections that I have found specifically helpful in looking at schools. From Houston, Texas, and the fine work of Waltrip High School and their district support I learned the questions from Josephine Rice: "What? So what? Now what?" Basically, what is in evidence—what do we see? What are the implications for this in our work and for the lives of students in our schools? And what are we going to do to change practice, to improve?

I urge you to push deeply in discussions. Too often we are able to state, for example, "we will have personalized learning environments for our students" without being able to articulate what that would mean. My friends and colleagues Josephine Rice and Trish McNeil have a great knack for this and have taught me to push more deeply, to not accept the surface answers. What would "it" look like? How would you know if it was real? What would it take to get there?

Frank Cruse, department chair and Small Learning Community coordinator at Waltrip, taught me a simple evaluation matrix. What are we doing well? What are we barely doing? What are we not doing at all? It sets us up for what we need to do next.

In addition to these questions, I have found the reflections posed by my friend and colleague from High Schools That Work, Heather Sass, useful in gaining feedback and paying attention to the subtleties of this work. They include the following: I am glad to see . . . ; I am concerned about . . . ; I want to make sure we include. . . . These will serve as a useful guide to end each study section.

Throughout this guide you will see those questions and reflections come together in the following manner. They come together as four broad sections for study under each chapter.

- ***Essential Questions for Discussion***. In each of the "essential questions" sections, I have posed questions that I used to help frame the chapter and ones I think are critical for groups to wrestle with to reach an understanding and, hopefully, consensus on their beliefs.
- ***Guiding Questions and Reflections***. In each "guiding question and reflection" section, I have posed questions that I believe you will need to grapple with if you are going to go deeply into this work.
- ***Activities***. These activities will provide opportunities to document what is in place and set priorities.
- ***Action Checklists***. Throughout the study process, from essential questions to the action checklist, you will be discovering strengths and deficits, looking at policies and practices, and setting in place actions you will want to take. This section of the guide provides three opportunities. First, the opportunity to codify the work of the discussions and decisions. Second, the opportunity to refer to and review the summary points at the end of each chapter. (You will notice that after Chapter 1, the bullet points in the summary sections change from observations to action items. You will review these and determine what you are doing, what you want to be doing, and what you will commit to do.) Last, you will use what I refer to as "the Heather Questions," noted earlier, to reflect on and summarize your efforts.

Now the work begins.

Chapter 1: The Battle Begins

Essential Questions for Discussion

- Should our schools, as they currently are structured, continue to exist?
- If they should change, why change and to what?
- Where are we in the process of reform?
- Are we clear on what "it" is we are trying to create?
- Do we believe "it" can really happen? For all students?
- Do we have consensus on this?
- If culture is a commonly held set of beliefs that results in shared practices, automatic responses, and ways of operating, doing our jobs, and responding to needs, how would we describe the culture of our organization?

Guiding Questions and Reflections

- Is the image of the hamster wheel one you can resonate with? Why or why not? What evidence of the hamster wheel phenomenon do you see in your work?
- Does a specific moniker—change, reform, reinvention, redesign, conversion—matter, or is it really about continuous improvement? Does what you call it enhance or detract from engagement of stakeholders? Does what you call it speak to the level of the need for improvement?
- Every school, every system has "those" students—perhaps they are children of poverty or color; perhaps they are new to American schools, or they may have special needs; they may be from "across the river" or "the other side of the tracks." Too frequently, they are underserved. They are often identified as the cause of the need for reform—because they have changed a community's heretofore traditional population. Sometimes educators feel that the reforms should be only for this group and the rest of the school can stay the same. Who are "those" children in your school or system? What do you observe about them; what is their impact on the educational delivery system? Are there implications in this that need to affect your work?
- What role does equity play in your discussion of school reform?
- *Breaking Ranks I* calls for schools to "unabashedly advocate for young people." What evidence do you see of that in your school/ system?

- *Breaking Ranks II* focuses on three core areas, the first of which is "sowing the seeds for change through collaborative leadership, professional learning communities, and the strategic use of data." Where do you see yourself as sower of seeds? How effective are you?
- Tony Wagner states that schools aren't failing; they simply haven't changed and the world has. Linda Darling-Hammond states that most people believe that our educational system is failing. She further states that it is because it is rigid and bureaucratic and wasn't designed to teach all children effectively, and now we have a mandate to do just that. Thomas Toch puts forth an impressive list of historical and current aspects of the American high school and notes their impact. What importance do these statements have for the reform process in your organization?

Activities

1. In Chapter 1, I explain that my organization looks at all reform work through a lens of just five broad areas, "the Big 5" of data-driven management, creating personalized communities for teaching and learning, having a laser-like focus on a high standards curriculum, developing strong partnerships, and creating a climate for success. In terms of the first four, what are you doing well, what are you barely doing, what are you not doing at all, what do you need to do?

	Doing well	Barely doing	Not doing	Need to do
Data				
Personalization				
High expectations curriculum				
Partnerships				

What *evidence* do you see related to how you rated these areas?
What would it look like if you were doing "it" well?

2. In terms of the fifth critical element, a climate for success, what are you doing well, what are you barely doing, what are you not doing at all, what do you need to do?

	Doing well	Barely doing	Not doing	Need to do
Clear mission and vision				
Achievable/aligned school plans				
Appropriate professional development				
Shared and empowered leadership				
Commitment to continuous improvement				
Climate of respect for students and staff				

What *evidence* do you see related to how you rated these areas?
What would it look like if you were doing "it" well?

3. *USA Today* conducted a research study on "school day doldrums" in which 11% of students reported that "every day in school is a bad day." What evidence of student satisfaction do you have at hand? Create a list of climate questions, conduct a student climate survey, and conduct focus groups. Invite a wide range of students to your study group and ask them to talk with you.

Action Checklist

Review the summary bullets at the end of the chapter. Are there any elements that need your particular attention? Any areas that need further discussion?

Review what you've covered in these discussions and activities. Document the "what, so what, and now what."

What?	So what?	Now what?

In terms of this discussion, and as a way to debrief this unit of study, share your reflections through the lens of "I am glad to see," "I'm concerned about," and "I want to make sure we include." Document what worked well, what was helpful, and what positive areas of work or practices were observed. Be as forthright in documenting the areas of discussion and practice that are of concern to you. Finally, as you move forward with planning and working, there are things that you will want to document to ensure they are included in any subsequent steps.

I'm glad to see	I'm concerned about	I want to make sure we include

Chapter 2: The Skunk Is on the Table

Essential Questions for Discussion

- Is your discussion open and honest? Are you operating in an atmosphere in which the skunks are dealt with, or is there a lack of trust or other barrier that keeps you from having hard discussions?
- Does your mission statement reflect what you believe about education and what today's students need to know and be able to do?
- Do you have an absolute commitment to put in place the policies and practices that you need to meet your mission?
- Do you know your data? What data is important? Who knows what? Who needs to know?
- What types of schools need to reform? When do we know when we are good? Can good schools become great?
- What is your compelling need to change?

Guiding Questions and Reflections

- Chapter 2 addresses the cycle of high hopes around new initiatives and the all-too-frequent dashing of those hopes as people get stretched, frustrated, tense, hurt, and the like. What evidence do you have of this in your organization? What can you do to minimize this cycle?
- What does "trust" look like in terms of reform?
- Does the cycle of programs, reforms, and staffing provide teachers with an excuse not to change? Why or why not?
- What do you think the level of frustration, fatigue, tension, and anger is among those you are seeking to involve in the reforms? Is it justified? What can be done to address this?
- What evidence do you have of your mission statement being central to how you operate? Is it the right mission statement?
- Are there state or district policies or initiatives that are impacting or will impact your reform work?

Activities

1. Sadly, the hamster wheel phenomenon resonates with many people both in their work and personal lives. What evidence of hamster wheel practices are in place in your work? What impact do those practices have? What are you going to do about them?

What?	So what?	Now what?

If you are really honest, are you *whirring?* Do you feel disempowered to change the system? Have you done what I described in Chapter 1—did you jump on the hamster wheel along with everyone else?

2. Too often in education we have a "disconnect" between mission, policy, and practice. Beginning to minimize the "disconnects" leads to coherency of practice and success, which leads to great engagement of stakeholders. In terms of the disconnects between your mission and your practices, what are you doing well, what are you barely doing, what are you not doing at all, what do you need to do?

	Doing well	Barely doing	Not doing	Need to do
Hiring practices				
Professional development and training				
How professionals relate to each other				
The texts used in classes				
Assessment of learning				
Standards movement				
Teacher preparation				
How parents and partners are engaged				
How we relate to students				

What *evidence* do you see related to how you rated these areas?
What would it look like if you were doing "it" well?

3. To succeed in changing outcomes for students, teacher practice, both in the classroom and in joint practice, needs to change. Is this an accurate statement? Below is a list of practices that should be at the core of good teaching. Is the list complete? What are your teachers doing well, barely doing, not doing at all, need to do?

	Doing well	*Barely doing*	*Not doing*	*Need to do*
Participating in learning communities that look at data to guide practice and instruction				
Developing plans that are attainable				
Refining their skills				
Succeeding with students				
Studying together and sharing their practices				
Redefining their profession				
Receiving recognition				

What *evidence* do you see related to how you rated these areas?
What would it look like if you were doing "it" well?

4. Chapter 2 presents a sobering set of statistics on student outcomes. It also deals honestly with whole-school data by highlighting the "quiet secret" of Hackensack, New Jersey, where "the failure to meet the needs of all our students is masked by a relatively impressive list of academic accomplishments on the part of our thriving students. Lift the mask and you see an underserved population whose members receive multiple D's and F's every grading period." Conduct a data review. Chart out the results.

a. Compare your statistics to those listed in Chapter 2.

b. Is the Hackensack example relevant to your school/district?

c. What other data do you want to know about?

d. What is your student attendance rate? What is your teacher attendance rate?

e. What is your school/system's average GPA?

f. Are the number of AP courses increasing?

g. How else can you document rigor in classes?

h. How are your subpopulations doing in comparison to the rest of the school?

i. Which teachers are succeeding with which students?

j. Is a certain department, or a certain individual within a department, getting significantly different results with students? How do you know what that result means . . . is an A an A?

5. What should a graduate of your school/district look like? Create your ideal graduate. List the academic, skill, and character traits that you believe are essential for postsecondary success. Push yourself to "go deep," beyond the surface, beyond stated district guidelines and policies.

Ideal graduate		
Academic skills	Life skills	Character traits

Are you producing that now? In what specific percentages? What are the demographics of those students? What are you doing to ensure that all students meet these criteria? What would you have to do?

6. Will Daggett at International Leadership in Education has identified nine characteristics of schools that are meeting with success. What are you

doing well, what are you barely doing, what are you not doing at all, what do you need to do?

	Doing well	Barely doing	Not doing	Need to do
Evidence of characteristics of small, autonomous learning communities				
Evidence of high expectations				
9th-grade focus				
12th-grade focus				
Use of data				
Effective curriculum				
Supportive relationships/ reflective thought				
Effective professional development				
Evidence of leadership				

What *evidence* do you see related to how you rated these areas?
What would it look like if you were doing "it" well?

7. In order to create the good high school, seven habits have been suggested. Are these right? What's missing?

Seven habits of highly effective schools	Doing well	Barely doing	Not doing	Need to do
Demonstrates high expectations and a vision that matches them				
Builds capacity and creates a true climate for success				

Thinks small and dreams big				
Engages in legitimate community support				
Thrives with strong, sustained, shared leadership				
Effectively aligns and manages resources				
Understands time				

What *evidence* do you see related to how you rated these areas?
What would it look like if you were doing "it" well?

Action Checklist

Beginning in this chapter, the summary bullets move from observations to items for commitment and action. Review the list. Which of these are you already committed to and acting on? What needs further work?

Review what you've covered in these discussions and activities. Document the "what, so what, and now what."

What?	So what?	Now what?

In terms of this discussion, and as a way to debrief this unit of study, share your reflections through the lens of "I am glad to see," "I'm concerned about," and "I want to make sure we include." Document what worked well, what was helpful, and what positive areas of work or practices were observed. Be as forthright in documenting the areas of discussion and practice that are of concern to you. Finally, as you move forward with planning and working, there are things that you will want to document to ensure they are included in any subsequent steps.

I'm glad to see	I'm concerned about	I want to make sure we include

CHAPTER 3: D.U.C.K.S. COME IN F.L.O.C.K.S.

Essential Questions for Discussion

- Wheatley states, "There is no power for change greater than a community discovering what it cares about." What do you and your community care about? Are they the same things? How is that evidenced?
- How is the need for change communicated in a compelling manner to stakeholders? Is it?
- What does "engagement" or "buy in" look like?
- What do you want folks to buy into?
- Do we have the right people in the right jobs with the right commitment and the capacity?

Guiding Questions and Reflections

- Chapter 3 opens with the idea of "magic wand wishes," one set from administrators, one from teachers. Are these right? What factors play into the disparity between the two sets of wishes?
- Structures, instruction, and cultural norms all affect student outcomes. *Breaking Ranks II* positions each of these as critical to a reform process and states that without a change in culture the structural and instructional changes will not take hold. Discuss.
- Chinyelu Martin aptly describes the "educational landscape" of many of our youth. What is your landscape? Are the structures and practices in place reflective of that, or have you missed something that could ensure your and your students' success?
- Michael Fullan notes that surrounding yourself with "yes" people is "not a bad strategy for getting through the day, but a lousy one for getting through the implementation dip." Review your roster for school improvement. Who else should be at the table? Why?
- What does "capacity" look like? How do you create it? How do you know if it's real?
- Should all teachers have their own professional improvement plan? Who should help coach and monitor it? How should they be held accountable?
- Charles Sturdivant teaches us that when it comes to reforming our high schools, "there is no box." Is he right? Discuss. What are the implications for your work?

Activities

1. What are you doing well in terms of reform? School reform does not mean throwing the baby out with the bath water. Catalogue those efforts that you are doing well. Document what impact they are having on structure, climate, instruction, and student success.

What we are doing	Impact

2. Keller states, "If culture deals with how people perform their work, then changes in culture must involve new patterns of work." Take out the job descriptions of the study group, of principals, counselors, department chairs, and so on. Decide which elements make sense and contribute to the reform efforts and which detract or are extraneous. Are there ways to delete or realign tasks? What needs to be added? How will you gain consensus and approvals for revised descriptions? Is there one for teachers? Should there be?

3. Without naming names, or maybe you need to, identify your "ducks." Are they ducks because they have every right to believe that the reform is one more in a cycle of reforms? If so, what actions do you need to take?

    a. _____

    b. _____

    c. _____

    d. _____

    e. _____

Using the wisdom of LaFourche Parish schools, what professional development activities can be implemented to enable them to gain opportunities, creativity, knowledge, and skills?

D.U.C.K. trait	Professional development need

4. Student voice is too often lost in the process of reform. In addition to the focus group discussions mentioned above, have students create their "ideal teacher," similar to the "ideal student" creation earlier.

Ideal teacher		
What we want them to know	What we want them to do in class and in school	How we want them to treat us

Ask students how many of their current teachers would fall into this category—many, few, or none. Ask them how many would fall into this category over the course of their high school experience.

Chart out the results and share them with the faculty. What is their reaction? Be prepared for a healthy discussion. Ask them to identify ways in which they can change *their own* practice to get closer to the ideal.

5. There are many individuals working in schools who are there to support the reform/improvement efforts of educators. Create a list of partners

and consultants and their primary roles in reform. How are their services and their involvement *directly* related to furthering your mission? If they are not, why are they there? Should they be involved in more meaningful and substantive ways, or should the resources that keep them involved be redirected to more effectively meet your mission?

How do they support "the big 5" of data-driven management, creating personalized communities for teaching and learning, having a laser-like focus on a high standards curriculum, developing strong partnerships, and creating a climate for success?

Are the partners and consultants aware of each other's efforts, and are they working together? If not, make this an action item!

Action Checklist

Review the summary bullets at the end of the chapter. Which of these are you already committed to and acting on? What needs further work?

Review what you've covered in these discussions and activities. Document the "what, so what, and now what."

What?	So what?	Now what?

In terms of this discussion, and as a way to debrief this unit of study, share your reflections through the lens of "I am glad to see," "I'm concerned about," and "I want to make sure we include." Document what worked well, what was helpful, and what positive areas of work or practices were observed. Be as forthright in documenting the areas of discussion and practice that are of concern to you. Finally, as you move forward with planning and working, there are things that you will want to document to ensure they are included in any subsequent steps.

I'm glad to see	I'm concerned about	I want to make sure we include

CHAPTER 4: GLASS BALLS AND HEDGEHOGS

Essential Questions for Discussion

- What do you hold sacred? What are your "glass balls"? Do you have agreement on this?
- What does your organization have a laser-like, hedgehog focus on? Is it the "main thing"?
- What is leadership?
- Who leads whom?
- Who, then, is responsible for change and improvement?

Guiding Questions and Reflections

- What does personal accountability mean? How can that be displayed in the context of this study and reform process?
- Covey relates a frightening set of statistics to a soccer team's ability to perform. How would you catalogue or quantify your own organization using this analogy?
- In this chapter, I highlight a perhaps not-so-mythical district. How does your district compare? What has kept the good work going? What has made it slow to a stop?
- Michael Fullan talks about an "implementation dip." I talk about an implementation *crevasse*. Where are you on the spectrum between high performance, dipping, and falling into a crevasse? Why? How can you push past this?

Activities

1. In the text, and in one of the activities for Chapter 2, we have suggested that teachers should commit and change their practices to reflect the use of data, sharing best practices, reinventing themselves, and the like. I posit that a teaching core that commits to these practices should expect the three things noted in the table that follows. What are you doing well? What are you barely doing? What are you not doing at all? What do you need to do?

	Doing well	Barely doing	Not doing	Need to do
Have in place a coherent set of practices and policies				
Hire staff that is aligned to the mission of the school				
Have school board support for work at the school level				

What *evidence* do you see related to how you rated these areas?
What would it look like if you were doing "it" well?

2. According to the Coalition for Essential Schools, "given [these] daunting new circumstances, schools now need every new leader they can get." Describe the characteristics of good leadership; note who should be able to demonstrate these traits.

What traits do we want from a leader?	What do we want a leader to do?	Who should have these characteristics?

Refer to the long list of leadership action items in this chapter. Are you in agreement? As leaders, how can you individually and collectively take ownership to see that these things are accomplished?

3. The plan is the thing. Perhaps the biggest stumbling blocks to effective reform are the competing initiatives, mixed messages, lack of aligned resources, and individual plans that are not connected one to another or to

the mission. Take out your school improvement plan, your action plan for your department, or any plans that relate to funding, accountability, goals and mission. Chart them out.

Plan or grant	Stated goals	Related to mission: yes/no/ somewhat	Supported by staff time and resources	Other notes
	1. 2. 3. 4.			
	1. 2. 3. 4.			
	1. 2. 3. 4.			
	1. 2. 3. 4.			

What are the implications of this for your work?

Action Checklist

Review the summary bullets at the end of the chapter. Which of these are you already committed to and acting on? What needs further work?

Review what you've covered in these discussions and activities. Document the "what, so what, and now what."

What?	So what?	Now what?

In terms of this discussion, and as a way to debrief this unit of study, share your reflections through the lens of "I am glad to see," "I'm concerned about," and "I want to make sure we include." Document what worked well, what was helpful, and what positive areas of work or practices were observed. Be as forthright in documenting the areas of discussion and practice that are of concern to you. Finally, as you move forward with planning and working, there are things that you will want to document to ensure they are included in any subsequent steps.

I'm glad to see	I'm concerned about	I want to make sure we include

CHAPTER 5: THE SIMPLE TRUTH

Essential Questions for Discussion

- Do we agree that we must change how we teach and how we manage schools?
- Are we motivated and committed enough to conquer the hamster wheel?
- Do we have what we need to succeed?

Guiding Questions and Reflections

- The retelling of the story of Eric captures both the importance of good teaching and what students have to teach us. Share stories of times when students taught you about the importance of teaching, kept you focused on what was important, and provided you with a reason to stay in education.
- Why, when we know what we want to create for our schools, is it so difficult to create the climate for success?
- What do we do that makes sense for children? What do we do that does not?

Activities

1. Margaret Thatcher credited Ronald Reagan with a strong set of characteristics that she believed made him effective. As they relate to your reform work, what are you doing well, what are you barely doing, what are you not doing at all, and what do you need to do?

	Doing well	*Barely doing*	*Not doing*	*Need to do*
Know what you want				
Act decisively				
Acknowledge your role and others as leaders				
Have resolve and stay focused on the mission				
Never shrink from the task				
Develop strategies to carry everyone along				
Know what you stand for				

What *evidence* do you see related to how you rated these areas?
What would it look like if you were doing "it" well?

Checklist

Review what you've covered in these discussions and activities. Document the "what, so what, and now what."

What?	*So what?*	*Now what?*

In terms of this discussion, and as a way to debrief this unit of study, share your reflections through the lens of "I am glad to see," "I'm concerned about," and "I want to make sure we include." Document what worked well, what was helpful, and what positive areas of work or practices were observed. Be as forthright in documenting the areas of discussion and practice that are of concern to you. Finally, as you move forward with planning and working, there are things that you will want to document to ensure they are included in any subsequent steps.

I'm glad to see	I'm concerned about	I want to make sure we include

Plans are only good intentions unless they immediately degenerate into hard work.

—Peter Drucker

Printed in the United States
By Bookmasters